MINING

Mining

The History of Mining in British Columbia

By G.W. Taylor

hancock house

Copyright © 1978   Geoffrey Taylor
ISBN 0-919654-87-8

Taylor, Geoffrey W., 1905-
   Mining

(The Resource series)
Bibliography: p.
Includes index.
ISBN 0-919654-87-8

1. Mineral industries—British Columbia—
History. I. Title. II. Series.
HD9506.C23B78 338.2'09711 C77-002157-3

Designed by NICHOLAS NEWBECK DESIGN

Published by:

Hancock House Publishers Ltd.

3215 Island View Road
SAANICHTON, B.C. V0S 1M0

Hancock House Publishers Inc.

12008 1st Avenue South
SEATTLE, WA. 98168

Contents

The Mine Finders

Introduction by Thomas Elliott

During my 47 year association with the mining industry in western Canada, the largest part of which was spent with the British Columbia & Yukon Chamber of Mines, it was my privilege to witness the discovery of most of the present producing mines and those that will be producers during the years ahead. My job with the Chamber placed me in the position of becoming personally acquainted with many of the prospectors, geologists, and other professional people responsible for the mineral discoveries. I also became familiar with the small and large mining companies that provided most of the risk capital so essential to this important endeavor.

At the outset, I wish to emphasize one important fact. Mineral discoveries are made by inspired, intelligent, determined people, not by the bureaucratic government type of organizations that are, in some parts of Canada, now being promoted as the answer to the current decline in prospecting activity. Academic theorists, who are today evident in some socialistically inclined government circles, are endeavoring to encourage the belief that regardless of what happens to the private sector, they can be counted on to uncover the mineral resources that lie buried beneath the surface of this vast and often inhospitable land. Nothing could be further from the truth!

The second point I wish to make is that the majority of our producing mines, and those that have gone before, were found and developed by the combined efforts of a great many people from different walks of life. It is seldom that the creation of a mine can be attributed to the efforts of one man, or, for that matter, to the efforts of one company. In other words, the often heard statement that "mines are made, not found," is to a large degree correct.

7

The third interesting fact is that in so many instances the discovery of mineral deposits occurs as a result of an unusual set of circumstances, sometimes by a "fluke"; and that, in my opinion, is what makes the searching for new mines such an interesting and challenging profession. A person never really knows where the next important mineral discovery will be made! One could have obtained the best professional and scientific advice regarding the mineral potential of a particular area but, as history has shown, "Mother Nature" has a habit of changing the rules and placing valuable ore deposits in the most unlikely locations. Scientific advances in the fields of geology, mineralogy, geophysics and geochemistry have contributed much to man's ability to locate mineral deposits but they are, after all, only aids to the prospector or geologist working in the field.

Development of the geiger counter used in the search for uranium ores was a notable achievement in providing a "tool" that actually caused this radio-active mineral to "speak" (by clicks on the counter) of its presence beneath the overburden. Again, the fluorescent lamp made it possible for a prospector, working in the dark, to see scheelite, a valuable ore of tungsten, that is often hidden from the naked eye. There are a number of other modern "tools" such as the diamond drill for probing beneath the earth's surface; the bulldozer for removing overburden; and the helicopter for moving men and materials into remote areas. In some instances, dogs have been trained to "smell" mineral deposits by sniffing out mineral oxidation near the surface.

The fourth, and possibly the most important point to be emphasized, is that by far the majority of mineral discoveries are made by prospectors and small public "stock" companies. During the past year I completed a study of who was responsible for the original discovery of seventy mineral deposits listed in the annual "Exploration Review" of the British Columbia and Yukon Chamber of Mines. This study revealed a fact I had always known; namely, that at least eighty-five per cent of these deposits were originally discovered by the prospector and/or the small mining company. Obviously then, the need to encourage the training and activities of prospectors, and the formation of small public "stock" companies, should be apparent to all.

Unfortunately, during the past number of years, Federal and Provincial Government legislation has been so designed as to discourage both prospectors and small companies. Taxation by the Federal Government of a prospector's "once in a lifetime gain" from the sale of his mineral discovery was a highly retrogressive step as it removed the incentive that had encouraged men to devote their lives to the heart-breaking task of uncovering nature's hidden wealth. Furthermore, the tax on capital gains, coupled with increasingly stringent securities legislation and rising costs of administration, caused many important entrepreneurs to quit the mining field and turn to other more rewarding lines of endeavor. It is ironic to note that after helping to "kill off" prospecting, the Federal and some Provincial Governments, are conducting public lotteries, the lucky winners of which are tax exempt!

As I have previously mentioned, the discovery and development of mines is the result of the combined efforts of a great many people. While I have already given credit to the prospectors and/or small companies for making most of the original discoveries, I would be remiss if I did not acknowledge the important role played by the major mining companies and their highly trained professional staffs. The normal sequence is that the initial mineral showing is found by the prospector, who then arranges a deal with a small company to explore the deposit. At a certain stage when a "showing" of some promise has been indicated, the property is "dealt off" to a major company that possesses the large sums of risk capital and technical "know how" to complete the job of developing the deposit and, if sufficient ore is found, of placing the mine into production. Today, many large companies also hire prospectors and geology students to search for new properties.

Recognition should be given to some branches of the Provincial and Federal Governments for the excellent work they have and are doing to aid in the search for new mines. Of particular importance are services rendered by the Geological Survey of Canada in publishing reports and maps that help to guide prospectors into promising areas. It is a known fact that a number of mines have been "found" by prospectors reading old geological reports or the Annual Reports of the B.C. Minister of Mines. Knowledge of mineral deposits and value of metals change throughout the years, sometimes causing an unattractive prospect to become a valuable ore deposit.

The current recession in prospecting and mine development in Canada is largely the result of unfavorable government legislation, particularly in the area of taxation. Introduction of a socialistic philosophy into our society and the erroneous belief that governments can do the "mine finding" and "mine operating" job as effectively as the private sector has destroyed the confidence of prospectors and investors. The special talents of this important group of men and the availability of large amounts of risk capital are essential to the future of our industry. It is to be hoped that governments, in their wisdom, are at last beginning to recognize this important fact.

Thomas Elliott
Mining Consultant
Vancouver, B.C.

Late Secretary-Manager
B.C. Yukon Chamber of Mines

10   *In the time of the Fraser River gold rush, the daily routine of thousands— panning for gold.*

1

A Golden Future

Gold has gripped the imaginations of men for thousands of years. Its color and malleability have made it particularly valuable for ornamentation. Two other factors enhanced its value: its relative scarcity and the ease with which placer gold could be extracted from the sand or gravel of rivers and streams, or from the crevices of surface rocks. Its durability and attraction made it ideal as a base for the value of other commodities. As a medium of exchange it became a symbol of wealth. Untold millions saw it as representing the material things of the world in the most desirable form.

By the nineteenth century gold had become accepted as a powerful instrument by the business communities of the great western trading nations. The fortunate possessors could command property, services and merchandise denied to those without it. After Britain went on the gold standard in 1821, gold became used more and more in business transactions. By the end of the century almost every country in the world (other than Mexico and China) had converted from silver to the gold standard. The lure of gold was unlimited and almost universal.

Gold rushes provided the most dramatic stories of the mining history of the last century. They started with discoveries in California in 1849, then in Australia in 1851, British Columbia in 1858, the Transvaal in 1886, and then . . . on to the Klondike in 1898. Consequences were profound in the areas involved. Two of the most important were the influx of thousands of gold-seekers and the opening up of the regions to western technology. Most of those engaged in the search were adventurers and transients; when the surface diggings were worked out they left for other places. With the possible exception of work in the Transvaal, gold mining did not become an industry supported by large capital outlays and sophisticated mining machinery until long after the surface diggings had been exhausted. But the rushes left behind one important piece of technology: a communications network of steamers, wagon roads and trails, and the nucleus of a population engaged in the basic needs of agriculture, commerce and government.

Consider the gold rush into the Fraser and Thompson rivers within its North American setting. In the mountains and rivers of the Far West were hidden gold and other minerals in greater profusion than had ever been dreamed of. The first great discovery came in 1848 in northern California. The rush brought thousands to the Pacific coast. A few became rich; many who were not so fortunate got the gold fever and with mule and shovel and washing pan started to search throughout the vast West. They made their way through northern California and Oregon, and over into the Inland Empire in Washington Territory. It was not accidental that they should eventually find themselves on the banks of the Thompson River and the creeks that fed it.

As they moved northward they carried with them their mining techniques and their accustomed ways of life. To the rivers and creeks of southern B.C. they brought their characteristic looks and attire: an unshaven jaw, long hair, a face wrinkled by years of outdoor living, a colored flannel shirt, high boots and an old hat. It all pinpointed a miner whether he was from Colorado, Nevada, California, Oregon or the Fraser River. The rush to the Fraser and Thompson rivers in 1857 and '58 was just one episode in the continuing story of the development of the American Far West.

The first known discovery of gold in British Columbia was reported in 1850. Richard Blanshard, the first governor of Vancouver Island, wrote to Earl Grey, the Colonial Secretary in London, in August of that year that he had seen "a very rich specimen of gold ore said to be brought by the Indians of Queen Charlotte's Island." In the following year a nugget weighing five ounces was offered in trade to the Hudson's Bay factor at Fort Simpson. Reportedly it had been found by an Indian woman on the beach at Moresby Island. In another despatch to Earl Grey (on March 29, 1851), Governor Blanshard wrote, "I have heard that fresh specimens of gold have been obtained from the Queen Charlotte islanders; I have not seen them myself but they are reported to be very rich."

Chief Factor James Douglas at Fort Victoria, where the gold had been sent, decided to send up the Hudson's Bay Company brigantine *Una* to investigate. She made two trips, one in July and the other in October of 1851, to Mitchell Harbour. On this second trip she was lost. But despite interference by the Indians a quartz vein seven inches wide and traceable for eighty feet was uncovered. The news quickly spread southward into the Puget Sound country and two U.S. vessels sailed for the Queen Charlottes. They remained only a few days. One of the vessels was wrecked and the crew taken prisoner. The other returned to Puget Sound for more arms and reinforcements before the crew rescued their compatriots. From a gold-finding standpoint the excursion was clearly a failure.

One of the greatest obstacles to the gold-seekers in the Queen Charlottes was the hostility of the natives. The Indians early realized the value that white men attached to these yellow pebbles. They reasoned that the Hudson's Bay trader would give them good value in exchange, so whenever they found gold they would bring it to a Hudson's Bay post. White men coming into their territory looking for gold were very much resented as reported by Chief Trader W.H. McNeill in a letter from the *Una* to James Douglas:

> I am sorry to inform you that we were obliged to leave off blasting and quit the place for Fort Simpson on account of the annoyance we experienced from the natives. They arrived in large numbers say thirty canoes and were much pleased to see us on our first arrival. When they saw us blasting and turning out the gold in such large quantities they became excited and commenced depredations on us, stealing our tools and taking at least one half of the gold that was thrown out by the blast. They would lie concealed until the report was heard then make a rush for the gold; a regular scramble between them and our men would then take place; they would then take our men by the legs and hold them away from the gold . . The natives were very jealous of us when they saw that we could obtain gold by blasting; they had no idea that so much could be found below the surface; they said that it was not good that we should take all of the gold away; if we did so they would not have anything to trade with other vessels should any arrive. In fact they told us to be off.

Victoria, circa 1860.

Commander R.C. Mayne, "Four Years in British Columbia"

The *Una* party consisted of only eleven men, so McNeill thought it prudent to withdraw.

When news of the discoveries reached San Francisco six vessels were equipped; in April and May of 1852 they sailed for the northern waters, but experienced little success in the Queen Charlottes and quickly returned southward. In the meantime the Hudson's Bay Company had purchased a U.S. ship that had gone on the rocks outside Esquimalt. It repaired her and renamed her the *Recovery*. Under a co-operative agreement with a group of thirty miners she sailed in March 1852 for the Charlottes under the Hudson's Bay flag. Three months were spent in Mitchell Harbour, amassing gold ore for shipment to be refined in England. (Eventually it turned out that each miner had earned only a dollar a day for his endeavors.)

James Douglas was one of the remarkable men-on-the-spot from the United Kingdom who appeared in the nineteenth century to take control in critical periods of expansion within the British Empire. Born (it is said) in Demerara, British Guiana, he was taken to Scotland at an early age. He came out to Canada as an apprentice with the North West Company and was sent to the Pacific coast soon after its amalgamation with the Hudson's Bay Company. For forty-five years he served there, ultimately becoming head of all Hudson's Bay activities on the Pacific slope. A man of outstanding ability, he soon rose to positions of command. His autocratic traits, developed through the exercise of absolute power, served Britain and the company well in the dangerous days of the Fraser River gold rush. Training and experience — to say nothing of a massive build — gave him the dominant role in events that culminated in the formation of British Columbia. He had seen the first American settlers trek into Oregon and break his company's long-established hold. He saw similar events developing in the Queen Charlottes and took steps to prevent them. He knew at first hand of the effects of the discovery of gold on an undeveloped country with no organized government. He also knew that as the news spread there would be no hope of stopping a rush of strong-willed men with scant respect for laws and regulations. When the rush came, he was ready. Ways were found to establish law and order and to maintain the British connection.

James Douglas was now wearing two hats — one as the chief executive officer of the Hudson's Bay Company at Victoria, the other as Governor of the British Crown Colony of Vancouver Island. The Colonial Secretary, Sir John Parkington, in September 1852 commanded Douglas "to take immediate steps for the protection of British interests against the depredations of the Indians and the unwarranted intrusions of foreigners on the territory of the Queen" in the new colony of the Queen Charlottes. Accompanying the instructions was a Queen's commission making James Douglas Lieutenant-Governor of the "Colony of Queen Charlotte's Island."

A great colonial administrator in the days of the Fraser River gold rush: Sir James Douglas.

In honor of one of the greatest British Columbians. The monument to Sir James Douglas on the grounds of the Parliament Buildings in Victoria, B.C.

Facsimile of letter dated August 24, 1852, from James Douglas to Joseph McKay, authorizing him to proceed to Nanaimo and "take possession" of coal beds lately discovered— in behalf of the Hudson's Bay Company.

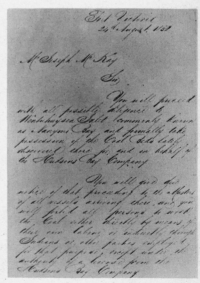

Nanaimo, from the Anchorage, circa 1860.

In March 1853 Governor Douglas in this new capacity issued a proclamation asserting the right of the Crown to any gold found on the islands. This was the first important step in the evolution of the mineral industry in British Columbia. For the first time it was publicly announced that gold and eventually all minerals in the ground in the Pacific possessions of British North America came under government ownership. This was followed in April by another proclamation setting up a system of miners' licenses. To seek or process gold ore, miners would now be liable for a monthly fee of ten shillings — the fee payable in advance, the license obtainable only at Victoria.

The mini-rush to the Queen Charlottes petered out, but it proved to be of historical importance — if only through making the Hudson's Bay Company officials gold-conscious. It set precedents that proved invaluable when invoked by Governor Douglas in the greater rushes that were to occur on the Fraser and Thompson rivers. It was on the Queen Charlottes that James Douglas in his capacity as governor asserted the traditional rights of the Crown to all discoveries of precious metals. He also took the first steps toward government regulation of miners and mining, an approach that was to have far-reaching results in the mining districts of the Fraser and Cariboo.

All the earlier samples of gold found in British Columbia came by way of trade into the possession of the Hudson's Bay Company. The agent at Kamloops obtained gold dust from the Indians as early as 1852. According to Douglas, writing in 1860:

> Gold was first found on Thompson's River by a Indian, a quarter of a mile below Nicoamen. He is since dead. The Indian was taking a drink out of the river. Having no vessel he was quaffing from the stream when he perceived a shining pebble which he picked up and it proved to be gold. The whole tribe forthwith began to collect the glittering metal.

Roderick Finlayson, another Hudson's Bay employee, says that in 1855 or 1856, the Indians discovered gold in rock crevices on the banks of the Thompson. Donald McLean, in charge of the post at Kamloops, inspected the gold-bearing ground and asked Victoria to send up some iron spoons so that the natives could extract the gold from rocks in the beds of the creeks. The spoons were sent up with instructions from Victoria to encourage the Indians in their endeavors and to take gold in trade whenever offered.

Further to the south, Angus McDonald reported to Victoria from Fort Colville that gold had been found in the valley of the Columbia just south of the Canadian-U.S. border. This was reported by Douglas to Henry Labouchere, Colonial Secretary, in his despatch of April 16, 1856. All that summer the rumor factory was busily circulating reports among the Indians and company employees. James Cooper, a witness testifying before a House of

Commons select committee looking into the Hudson's Bay Company affairs in London in 1857, linked the finding of gold at Fort Colville very closely with its discovery on the Thompson River. Dr. George M. Dawson of the Geological Survey of Canada held similar views. Writing in 1889 on the mineral wealth of British Columbia he said:

> It seems certain that the epoch-making discovery of gold in British Columbia was the direct result of the Colville excitement. Indians from the Thompson River visiting a woman of their tribe who was married to a French Canadian at Walla Walla spread the report that gold like that found at Colville occurred also in their country and in the summer and autumn of 1857 four or five Canadians and half-breeds crossed over to the Thompson and succeeded in finding workable placers nine miles above its mouth. On return of these prospectors the news of the discovery of gold spread rapidly.

In the summer of 1857 a few U.S. prospectors were entering the Thompson country from the south. In a despatch to the Colonial Office dated July 15 of that year Douglas wrote:

> A new element of difficulty in exploring the gold country has been interposed through the opposition of the native Indian tribes of Thompson's River, who have lately taken a high handed though possibly not unwise course of expelling all parties of gold diggers composed chiefly of persons from the American territories who had forced an entrance into their country. They have also openly expressed a determination to resist all attempts at working gold in any of the streams flowing into Thompson's River both from a desire to monopolize the precious metal for their own benefit and from a well-founded impression that the shoals of salmon which annually ascend those rivers and furnish the principal food of the inhabitants will be driven off and prevented from making their annual migrations from the sea.

It is almost certain that the Indian tribes for a considerable time were able to keep the Americans out and to enjoy an almost complete mining monopoly in the Thompson River region. In a later despatch of December 27, 1857, Douglas described conditions in the upper country as reported to him by correspondents:

> It appears from . . . reports that the auriferous character of the country is becoming daily more extensively developed through the exertions of the native Indian tribes, who having tasted the sweets of gold finding are devoting much of their time and attention to that pursuit.

> They are however at present almost destitute of tools for moving the earth and washing implements for separating the gold from the earthy matrix and have therefore to pick it out with knives, or to use their fingers for that purpose; a circumstance which in some measure accounts for the small product of gold up to the

present time, the export being only about 300 ounces since the 6th of last October.

Even in the spring of 1858, when news of the rich bars of the lower Fraser was spreading like a prairie fire in the territories of Washington and Oregon and as far southward as San Francisco, white prospectors were few and far between in the upper country.

The few white men passing the winter at the diggings were mainly retired servants of the Hudson's Bay Company, who were obstructed by the Indians in all their attempts to search for gold. They were narrowly watched; whenever they did succeed in excavating to gold-bearing depth they were quietly hustled or crowded by the natives who then proceeded to reap the fruits of their labors. However, as Douglas wrote on April 6, 1858, it was "a circumstance highly honorable to the character of those savages that they have on all occasions scrupulously respected the persons and property of their white visitors, at the same time that they have expressed a determination to reserve the gold for their own benefit."

In the autumn and winter of 1857 the reputed wealth of the Thompson River mines created much excitement in the territories of Washington and Oregon. Governor Douglas seemed to be in no doubt that many from those parts would be coming up in the spring, and the expectation prompted him to issue the famous proclamation of December 28, 1857:

> (Concerning) all mines of Gold and all Gold in its natural state of deposit within the districts of Fraser River and Thompson River . . . whether in the lands of the Queen or of any of Her Majesty's Subjects. . .

> Now I James Douglas the Governor aforesaid on behalf of Her Majesty do hereby publicly notify and declare that all persons who shall take from any lands within the said District any Gold Metal or ore containing Gold or who shall dig for and disturb the soil in search of Gold Metal or ore without having been duly authorized in that behalf by Her Majesty's Colonial Government will be prosecuted both criminally and civilly as the Law allows.

> And I further notify and declare that such regulations as may be found expedient will be prepared and published setting forth the terms in which licenses will be issued for this purpose in payment of a reasonable fee.

The promised regulations were published the following day:

> From and after the first day of February next no person will be permitted to dig, search or remove gold or ore from any land public or private without first taking out and paying for a license.

Provision was made for setting up a "Commission" for carrying out these regulations and formulating rules for "adjusting the extent and position of land to be covered by each license."

Governor Douglas must have realized that there was no hope of averting a mad rush of Americans to the beckoning gold fields. His task was to exercise some administrative control and, even more important, to maintain British sovereignty over the territory. He therefore had the proclamations published in the newspapers of Washington and Oregon. Illegal though his acts were (his commission as Governor of the British Colony of Vancouver Island did not give him legal jurisdiction over the mainland), his assumption of authority was chiefly responsible for the fact that British sovereignty over these vast areas was never seriously questioned.

The earliest U.S. mention of the reported finds was in the *Pioneer and Democrat*, a weekly published in the little settlement of Olympia in Washington Territory. On March 5, 1858, the subscribers read:

> We learn from Captain Jones of the schooner *Wild Pigeon* who is engaged in freighting between this and other ports on the Sound and Strait with Victoria that much excitement exists on Vancouver Island in consequence of the alleged discovery of rich gold deposits to the northward in the British possessions. . . . According to representation they are located at Fort Hope and the Thompson River.

With the first signs of spring in 1858, some seventy or eighty Americans from Washington Territory appeared on the Fraser and started mining at Hill's Bar below Yale.

At the western entrance of the Fraser canyon. Site of the Fraser River gold rush. Yale as it appears today.

The switch that set off the starting gun in California was a rumor that the Hudson's Bay Company had sent a consignment of gold to the U.S. mint at San Francisco. (Such a shipment did arrive in April 1858 on the company's steamer *Otter*.) As Donald Fraser, the *London Times* correspondent, wrote: "None too poor and none too rich to go; none too young and none too old to go; even the decrepit go."

What kind of wilderness greeted the adventurers? It was a land of rugged mountains, of swift and dangerous rivers, of huge distances; its winter climate would test the hardiest and its native peoples were even less hospitable. There were no roads in British Columbia. The means that made any communication possible — canoes and barges and steamers over the waterways, mules and oxen and horses over the trails — were practically nonexistent except for the few in use by the Hudson's Bay Company. Stocks of food and implements still lay in the warehouses of the merchants of the eastern seaboard.

Before April was out, the U.S. steamship *Commodore* slipped into Esquimalt harbor one Sunday morning and landed 450 miners — doubling the population of Victoria in one day. Within a few weeks thousands more had arrived. The road from Esquimalt to Victoria became changed beyond recognition and in the words of Commander R.C. Mayne, "was covered with pedestrians toiling along with the step and air of men whose minds are occupied with thoughts of business . . . strangers of every tongue and country in every variety of attire."

A page from The Illustrated London News *of May 12, 1866, with line drawings of Yale and the Fraser River canyon, from a correspondent on the spot.*

In July the excitement in Victoria reached its climax. On July 1 the steamer *Sierra Nevada* landed 1900; a week later the *Orizaba* and *Cortez* brought another 2800. On Puget Sound all shipping became paralyzed. Crews deserted *en masse*. Sawmills and logging camps closed down through lack of help. Stores lay unattended, and some smaller settlements became deserted. No one knows how many tried to get to the diggings that summer, but the *Victoria Gazette* estimated that at least 25,000 people passed through Victoria.

Between the goldfields and Victoria lay 200 miles of water and bush. No conventional link was in existence. The would-be miners had to cross the Strait of Georgia by any means at hand; sailboat, rowboat, skiff, canoe or raft. Thousands succeeded in crossing but many perished in the attempt. Then the Fraser had to be navigated — a swift and dangerous stream. "Many accidents have happened in the dangerous rapids," wrote Douglas. "A great number of canoes have been dashed to pieces and their cargoes swept away by the impetuous stream while of the ill-fated adventurers who accompanied them many have been swept into eternity."

When the survivors arrived upstream in June and July the river was so high that the bars were under water and could not be worked. Thousands turned away to retrace their steps. Those who remained faced hostile Indians. On August 14 a pitched battle took place near Boston Bar between 150 angry miners and a band of Indians. The Indians were completely routed and left seven of their number dead. Douglas immediately set out for the mainland with the

A present-day scene on the Thompson River where, in 1857, a small number of Americans found gold.

B.C. GOVERNMENT

strongest millitary force he could muster including marines from *H.M.S. Satellite* and a few military personnel from the Boundary Commission. (The commission consisted of British and U.S. surveyors and scientists appointed by their respective governments to determine and mark the boundary from the Rockies to the Pacific, as agreed upon in the Oregon Treaty. Each group had a military escort.) His arrival at Hope on September 1 had a calming effect and one more crisis was averted.

On June 30 a Queen's Proclamation from Victoria provided new regulations for the miners. A license had to be carried on the person and produced when demanded by any commissioner, peace officer or other authorized person. The area of a miner's claim was spelled out: no more than twelve feet square. Provisions were made for parties of up to four, a number that was entitled to 576 square feet; no greater area was allowed on any one claim.

James Douglas never lost sight of the fact that he was also responsible for the affairs of the Hudson's Bay Company in the Pacific region. This was demonstrated by his proclamation of May 8, 1858:

> All ships, boats, and vessels together with the goods laden on board found in Fraser's River . . . not having a license from the Hudson's Bay Company and a sufferance from the proper officer of the Customs at Victoria shall be liable to forfeiture and will be seized and condemned according to law.

He backed up the order with the power of the British Navy. On his instructions *H.M.S. Satellite* was stationed off the mouth of the Fraser River to intercept any vessels contravening this decree.

Understandably, the miners were incensed by such regulations and sought to evade them. Settlements on Puget Sound vied with each other and with Victoria to attract potential travellers to the goldfields. The little hamlet of Whatcom on Bellingham Bay, thanks to her splendid harbor and her relative proximity to the mines, offered the greatest advantages. In April and May of 1858 thousands arrived and camped on the shores of the bay. Those who were awaiting means to get the mines held a mass meeting to raise money for a trail from the bay to Fort Hope. The proceeds enabled work to start immediately, using portions of an old Indian trail and striking up the Noosask River to a point near the present town of Huntingdon; the route went from there along the eastern side of Sumas Lake to the Chilliwack River and thence to the Fraser. According to the *Victoria Gazette* it was in daily use by July, even though 'the trail strikes the river about thirty miles below Fort Hope and then (the miners) have to get Indians to bring them up in canoes." But the trail ended nowhere near the diggings and it was extremely difficult without a boat to travel the remaining distance to Fort Hope. It was discovered to be a "hopeless proposition" — discouraged by such pessimistic reports, hundreds encamped around Whatcom returned home.

Throughout that summer, miners flocked by boat into Portland and worked their way up the Columbia or from Fort Nisqually into the interior to hit the Hudson's Bay Brigade Trail through the Okanagan. Joel Palmer, the first man to drive a wagon to the Thompson River, reported passing companies of 400 to 500 men on this route. From Walla Walla in Washington Territory a party of 160 with 400 animals broke through to Lytton at the junction of the Thompson and Fraser rivers.

When the waters receded on the Fraser in late July the sand bars became exposed and a period of frenzied activity began. The bars between Hope and Yale were jammed with miners. Douglas estimated that at least 10,000 were working on the bars below Yale. Some found good returns: on Hill's Bar three partners took out forty-six lbs. of gold. Many claims yielded fifty ounces per day.

Meanwhile, much thought was being given in London to the problems arising from the rapid and unexpected rush to the goldfields. Sir Edward Bulwer-Lytton, the new Colonial Secretary, introduced a bill at Westminster setting up the machinery to establish a Crown colony in the vast area known up to then as New Caledonia. Within a few weeks by the expressed wish of Queen Victoria the name had been changed to British Columbia. The bill was passed by the British Parliament in August 1858; on November 19 of that year British Columbia was officially born at a ceremony at Fort Langley with Sir James Douglas as governor.

The first mining season closed amid despondency. It was said that only one miner in 500 made wages and one in a thousand did well. Most of the profitable mining had been done in the autumn when the water level was at its lowest. Before that time some 4,000 of those who had reached the mines had left, most of them for San Francisco. Earlier widespread publicity had done its work too well.

Expectations had started to build ten years earlier when the drama of the '49ers in California caught the fancy of the reading public. In a time of rising literacy, magazines and newspapers were eager to acquire and print dramatic and sensational stories from faraway places. Donald Fraser, a Scotsman trained as a lawyer, covered the California scene from 1849 as a special correspondent for the London *Times*. When news began to circulate in San Francisco about the gold discoveries in the British possessions to the north he was instructed to go up to Victoria and investigate. He arrived in the summer of 1858 with an introduction to James Douglas from the British consul in San Francisco.

Fraser had a fine literary style and was a tireless reporter. In Victoria he interviewed miners, packers, businessmen, government officials, clergymen, and anybody else who knew or thought he knew about the mines and the Fraser and Thompson river countries. He would ask the hotel and lodging-house owners in Victoria to talk to their guests about their experiences in the fields and how much they had taken out in gold dust. This all resulted in the *Times* printing dramatic and highly readable accounts of splendid opportunities for getting rich quickly. The hardships and difficulties of the venture — the struggle to get to the mines, the often futile search for paydirt that would give an adequate return — were very much played down. Glowing descriptions of the wealth that could be acquired in the goldfields attracted a host of British immigrants. Many were totally unfitted for such a wild country. Hundreds came out with barely enough money to land them in the country. Many of the unfortunate souls stranded in Yale or New Westminster or Victoria harbored some bitter thoughts about Donald Fraser.

Present-day gold panning in the Fraser canyon near Yale.

B.C. GOVERNMENT

The writer took up residence in Victoria, building a house on Humboldt Street on property bought from the Hudson's Bay Company. Like other professional and business people in Victoria he started buying and selling real estate. He was appointed by Governor Douglas to the Executive Council of the Colony of Vancouver Island, and commuted between Victoria and San Francisco. Once the gold excitement of the Cariboo had subsided in 1866, he returned to London and never came back. Of his twenty-seven articles for the *Times* on the British Columbia scene, many were printed as pamphlets and enjoyed wide circulation in Eastern Canada and the United States. His writings, appearing in the most

24

influential of British newspapers, focused the attention of London decision-makers on the mineral and commercial possibilities of the two fledgling colonies.

Some U.S. newspapers had special correspondents sending despatches from the spot. In June 1858, despatches were being sent from the Fraser's sand bars to the *New York Times*. A month earlier a correspondent for the *San Francisco Bulletin* was writing on the findings at Hill's Bar. The publisher of the *San Francisco News* visited Victoria on the steamer *Cortes* to report on the situation and to establish a newspaper. Several books and guides for prospective immigrants came from the desks of San Francisco publishers as early as 1859. In England articles appeared very early in the monthly magazines (for example, *Fraser's Magazine* of October 1858) and the *Illustrated London News* offered pictures of scenes in the goldfields drawn by artists on the spot. Many books from London publishing houses added to the clamor.

One of the most interesting guides was compiled by Robert Ballantyne and published in Edinburgh in 1858. It contains descriptions (apparently at second hand) of the richness of the fields, the physical aspects of the country, and the best travel routes. This commercial success illustrates the keen interest shown by the Scottish reading public in the new goldfields.

Plaque erected on the site of the town of Douglas at the north end of Harrison Lake, the starting point of the Douglas-Lillooet Trail to the Cariboo.

Lillooet, a gateway to the Golden Cariboo.

By the autumn of 1858 U.S. steamers were sailing up the Fraser to the head of navigation at Yale or to Douglas at the northern end of Harrison Lake. The winter was coming on and most of the miners elected to go outside. The *Enterprise*, a U.S. sternwheeler carrying her last load of miners down river in mid-December, was caught in the ice somewhere below Hope and stuck there for three days. Many miners planned to sit it out in Victoria, no longer a tent town but much shrunk in population. Others stayed on the banks of Fraser in ill-constructed windowless cabins.

In the administration of government Douglas was now helped by a team of English officials carefully selected in London by the Colonial Secretary. One of these was Matthew Baillie Begbie,

25

View of Yale in 1966, showing the present Cariboo Highway.

A view of the Thompson River, on the banks of which native Indians first found gold.

sometimes called the "Hanging Judge." The fame of Mr. Justice Begbie and his British brand of justice spread far into the mining camps of the western United States. He would hold court anywhere — in a log shack, in a clearing in the forest or on horseback, always with an atmosphere appropriate to a British court of law. Immune to bribery, flattery or threats, he soon proved that the path of any troublemaker would be extremely hard. Governor Douglas held Judge Begbie in high regard. "Able, active, energetic and highly talented, Mr. Begbie is a most valuable public servant," he wrote in a confidential report submitted to the Colonial Office.

A detachment of Royal Engineers gave invaluable help in providing communications, in laying out trails and roads, in surveying land for mining titles or town lots. Under Col. R.C. Moody the 165 officers and men provided technical skills to open up the country to greater mineral exploration. In the coming days of prosperity, with the finding and opening of the rich Cariboo gold-mining country, they assisted in making wagon roads to the interior. The Cariboo wagon road through the Fraser Canyon ranks as one of the great road-building achievements of the nineteenth century. In the instructions given to Col. Moody by personal letter from Sir Edward Bulwer-Lytton the potential mineral wealth of the country was not overlooked. "You will remember," Sir Edward wrote, "that Gold is not the only mineral in which British Columbia is said to be rich. You will examine and report to Her Majesty's Government upon all its mineral productions." In the light of the many stories of fabulous wealth in this new land which were going the rounds in England, Sir Edward cautioned the colonel to be very careful to substantiate any information. "In this as in all mineral products of those districts," he wrote, "I entreat you to form the most dispassionate and careful judgement and rather own ignorance or doubt than ever to allow yourself to be misled by reliance on untested statements."

It was soon clear that the gold in the sand bars of the lower Fraser was only the start of a long line leading to a richer treasury in the interior. Most miners believed that richer deposits would be found as one ascended the river. The stumbling-block was the Fraser canyon. It was unsuitable for a mule trail and unnavigable for a boat. Some other route had to be found. The Indian trails through the canyons were, in the words of Judge Begbie, "utterly impassable for any animal but a man a goat or a dog." In rounding the cliffs, travellers had to walk on wooden poles put there by the Indians and suspended from above by deer-hide ropes. The arms of the traveller would be stretched out and his body kept as close to the rock as possible while the Fraser raged under his feet a thousand feet below.

The pressing problem now became how to get supplies beyond the canyons into the open spaces of the upper country. An acceptable route was found from Douglas at the head of Harrison Lake to

26

Lillooet on the Fraser.

The next two years saw many improvements to the Douglas-Lillooet route. Royal Engineers were put on the job at the southern end, and workers of J.W. Trutch (a civilian contractor who became the first Lietuenant-Governor of B.C.) undertook the middle and northern end. The portage trails were made into wagon roads twelve feet wide at a cost of $2,200 per mile under private contracting. Three sternwheelers built in Victoria were put on the lakes by private enterprises — the *Marzelle* on Lillooet Lake, the *Lady of the Lake* on Anderson Lake, and the *Champion* on Seton Lake. The route began at Port Douglas at the head of navigation on the northern end of Harrison Lake with a 29-mile road to Lillooet Lake, and from there a 22-mile drive brought the traveller to Anderson Lake. A mile-and-a-half road supplemented by a tramway joined Anderson to Seton Lake, only four miles from the Fraser at Lillooet. For several years until the completion of the Cariboo road from Yale this route carried the largest volume of traffic to the upper country. It stands in history as the first commercial route from the coast to the interior in gold-rush days. It gradually declined after 1863, unable to compete with the wagon road by way of the Fraser canyons. There were too many tolls and extra charges, and too much time and money went into trans-shipments.

To keep peace and order and sustain the presence of the government in an ever-expanding territory, Governor Douglas in 1859 devised and created a new breed of colonial officials named the Gold Commissioners: they were judges as well as the administrative officers of the government in mining districts and camps. All mining disputes under £50 were to be adjudicated by the commissioner without benefit of jury. He was empowered to make regulations for good governance of mining camps and communities within his district. As a magistrate and Justice of the Peace he was responsible for law and order within his jurisdiction. He issued miners' licenses, collected fees, registered mining claims, and acted as assistant commissioner of lands, collector of revenue, Indian agent, and electoral officer. In many districts he was the sole representative of the government, the one link between those who were governed and the officials in New Westminster or Victoria. In his selection of men for these positions Douglas demonstrated once again his ability to choose the right people. He turned to young men of adventurous frame of mind, with a good background and education, able to act on their own and to solve the problems of a pioneering country in an occasionally unorthodox way. Most of them were of Anglo-Irish extraction. The names of Peter O'Reilly, John Carmichael Haynes, A.C. Elliott, and William George Cox stand high among those who contributed to the building of this province.

The Anglican church at Yale, built in the 1860's by the Royal Engineers.

In 1858 the center of activity had lain between Hope and Yale. By 1859 miners trekked into the interior as the sand bars of the lower Fraser became played out. The center of activity moved north and east to the vicinity of Lytton. During that summer more than a thousand men were working the Fraser between Alexandria and Fort George. The march to Central British Columbia had begun.

Chinese prospector washing gold on Fraser River.

2

Cariboo Fever

In the Cariboo country, 1859 was the year of preparation. The Fraser River's bars below Yale were left to the industrious Chinese, who had followed the gold rushes from California. As soon as weather permitted navigation the more venturesome individuals pushed further up-stream through the canyon and on to Lytton and the junction with the Thompson. Some stayed and tried the benches around Lytton. Others hiked up the Thompson to its promising creeks — Tranquille, Nicola or Nicoamen — or tackled the Douglas-Lillooet trail as far as Cayoosh Creek or the Bridge River country. But the most fortunate were those who continued up the Fraser to its junction with the Quesnel. This point was reached in May 1859 and rich findings were gathered on such appropriately named bars as Rich and Britain. Miners prospected not only the banks of the Fraser but every creek and river that flowed into it from Lytton to 150 miles north of Fort George. By the summer of 1859 there were a thousand miners and prospectors in the upper country. A year later the total had jumped to three thousand.

Peter Curran and his party learned from an Indian of the existence of gold in the Lac La Hache country east of 150-Mile House. By June 1859 they were panning for gold on the Horsefly River and creating a minor rush as other parties flocked to stake their claims. At about the same time enough coarse gold was found on the Quesnel River to make several parties wealthy. On Snyder's Bar in that river three men recovered $1,000 worth of free gold in one day's work. All in all the season of 1859 proved eminently encouraging.

The following year continued the search eastward, into the creeks whose sources lay in the high lands around Bald and Agnes mountains. Some flowed south into Cariboo Lake, others northward to join the Willow or Bowron rivers. In a year's time they were to become known around the world as the famous Cariboo gold creeks — the richest plots of real estate in the Pacific Northwest.

When "Doc" Keithley and George Weaver made their strike on Keithley Creek at the southwest end of Cariboo Lake in the summer of 1860, practically all the gold-seekers in the upper country flocked to the scene. It was the first major find in this almost inaccessible region and unlocked the door to the mineral wealth of the Cariboo. In succession came findings on Snowshoe, Harvey, and Cunningham creeks. Many of the prospectors, not yet satisfied, pushed over the divide to find richer fields on creeks flowing to the north. In the fall of 1860, John Rose and Alex McDonald set out from Keithley Creek in search of new diggings. Ascending Keithley Creek for about five miles they set a course north up a ravine to Snowshoe Creek which they followed to its source near the summit of the watershed. From there they could see the heart of the Cariboo country: mountains upon mountains as far as the horizon. Here, although not always visible, were the creeks and valleys that would soon become the mecca of gold-seekers everywhere. Going over the summit they dropped into Antler Creek and found gold in abundance. They returned to Keithley Creek but could not keep silent and the location of their find became known. In the depth of a Cariboo winter hundreds started for Antler Creek to stake their claims. In some cases the same ground was staked by two or more parties and weapons were drawn. Word was sent to Philip Nind, the gold commissioner at Williams Lake, to come up and settle the disputed claims. On arrival he found one cabin built by the discoverers Rose and McDonald; "the rest of the miners were living in holes dug out of the snow which was between six and seven feet deep." He settled

The administrative capital of the Crown Colony of British Columbia in the Cariboo gold rush days. New Westminster as it looked in the 1860's.

the disputes and reported back to the Colonial Secretary at New Westminster. "The unsuccessful parties," he wrote, "submitted quietly on finding their claims were not supported by the law. It was patent to all who were old residents that English law if transgressed was not to be codded with the same impunity as California law." He further added that he felt things had gone so peaceably because the miners had a stake in the country and the prospects were so dazzling that nobody wished to jeopardize the future. The abundance of timber, he noted, would make the workings of the claims on Antler Creek easier and less expensive than any other known creek in the Cariboo.

30

In the same winter Edward Stout, Michael Burns and William Dietz crossed the ridge that leads up to the summit of Mount Agnes and descended upon the creek forming the headwaters of the Willow River, known to adventurers everywhere as Williams Creek. Here, halfway between what were to become Richfield and Barkerville, William Dietz found gold. The news spread rapidly and a mad rush started in the spring. Prospectors seeking a route came upon Lightning Creek which flows into the Swift River, and Lowhee Creek which empties into the Jack of Clubs Lake. In the spring and summer of 1860 others searched many creeks and found gold everywhere. Word of the richness of the finds spread like a prairie fire. The lower Fraser and Thompson became depopulated. The march was on to the Cariboo.

Williams Creek did not get into its stride until Jourdan and Abbott really began to dig into their claim and found gold-bearing gravel three or four feet below the surface. With three new partners the pair were soon taking out 120 ounces per day. Sir James Douglas reported that "they had a flour sack of gold fourteen inches high." That summer the whole creek and hillside above the canyon, a distance of six miles, was covered by miners and their claims. On Lightning Creek they had to go a little deeper, from eight to thirty feet, to strike paydirt. Ned Campbell's claim took out $100,000 in three months. On Lowhee the original findings were all shallow, with some of the richest ground in that locality yielding gold only four feet below the surface.

The richness of the Cariboo finds did not become generally known to the outside world until the next year, when the newspapers and magazines of Eastern Canada, the United States and Britain could not commission and print enough stories to satisfy the demand. Thousands, both rich and poor, decided to sell their homes and possessions and emigrate to British Columbia. By May 1862, some 6,000 gold-seekers had entered the Cariboo with 2,000 camped in the valley bottom and hillsides of Williams Creek. It has been estimated that in the Welsh coalfields in the spring of 1862, one out of every three in the working population had plans to emigrate to British Columbia. By then, in fact, some of the Welshmen had already arrived — people like David Grier, a partner in the rich Ericson claim. London's international fair of 1862 featured an exhibit furnished by the Colony of Vancouver Island and British Columbia which displayed "A Present from Cariboo — Three nuggets found and exhibited by Mr. David Grier, a miner in that goldfield."

Thousands of immigrants kept arriving at Victoria to find their way into the interior. The primitive conditions, the hardships and slowness of travel, and the exorbitant prices that had to be charged for food and supplies dampened enthusiasm, as explained in a letter written by a recent Welsh arrival in August 1862:

Six of us started from Victoria on the 3rd of June last for Cariboo . . . We travelled until we got within 100 miles of Cariboo where we halted and came to the determination that four of us should return to work on the roads and hand over all our spare cash to the other two, who were to go up and start 'prospecting.' This arrangement we of course made in consequence of the high price of provisions at the gold diggings. We (the four of us) worked on the road until August.

The almost insurmountable difficulties of building a wagon road through the Fraser canyon. Sailor Bar Bluff, 7½ miles north of Yale.

Thousands more who were arriving in the colony from Eastern Canada or the United States found themselves in the same predicament, with not enough money even to reach the gold fields. William Harris, who never arrived in the Cariboo, had seen the futility of the situation and returned to California. On January 24, 1863, he wrote to his family:

We met many men who had been there (the Cariboo) and had spent $500 but had found no gold. . . . But we saw men who had been there after this and had claims and gold and are going up again this year. There is gold to be had there but the great difficulty is to get hold of it. . . . Thousands have gone to the Cariboo with no money to stay there and there are some with claims from the previous year giving work to a few. But what is that in the face of the thousands that have gone and are going there. Each one who is short of money has to turn back as soon as they can. . . . There is no doubt that the Indians by their generosity have kept many alive on the way back and it is a three weeks walk before getting a boat for Victoria.

A well-organized attempt to bring out a party of gold-seekers from Britain was arranged by Henry Beecroft Jackson, a Manchester cotton manufacturer. Jackson agreed to finance a party of 26 for a period of two years. All expenses were to be paid by his agent in Victoria, Messrs. Janion, Green & Rhodes. A novel feature was the agreement to pay allowances to the wives and children of the members of the expedition left behind in England. John Evans, a close friend and former business associate of Jackson, was to select the men and lead the expedition into the field. He arrived in Victoria ahead of the party in April 1863 and looked over several locations, including the "Rich Bar" on the Fraser at Quesnel; through the co-operation of the gold commissioner and the miners on Lightning Creek, he was able to secure a lease on 2,500 feet on the bank of that creek including hillside and water rights. After the party arrived at Esquimalt, it made its way up-country along the Douglas-Lillooet route which was now passable for wagons. The trip was long, the roads were bad, and it was late in the summer when at last they reached Lightning Creek. Going up the steep hill over which the road climbs from the little settlement of Douglas, the men had to harness themselves in front of the horses before the wagons could reach the crest.

B.C. GOVERNMENT

A view of the ground in the Fraser canyon which posed such difficulties to the engineers laying out the Cariboo wagon road.

17 Mile Bluff, between Yale and Spuzzum on the Cariboo wagon road built in 1861. Note the extensive cribbing and wooden support-work necessary.

The story of this party, which spent two years in trying to develop its mine, is more typical than that of Billy Barker or "Cariboo" Cameron. As the group set up camp that autumn four men did nothing else but saw lumber for a projected water-wheel, sluice boxes, and shaft linings. They also had to build a house for winter quarters. A shaft was started but the water that dripped into it could be pumped out only with great difficulty. A major catastrophe could bring water in underground from the bottom and fill the whole shaft within half an hour. Makeshift pumps had to be made by boring holes through the centers of trees. Log pumps (as

33

they were called) had an unfortunate habit of bursting under pressure, and the greatest care had to be used when the shaft got down below 50 feet. Other devices were tried: for example, a canvas belt with a kind of scoop or wooden bucket attached which revolved around a drum at the shaft-head. The services of a strong miner were needed to wind up the drum. Evans continually complained that if he only had the use of the iron pumps found in the coal mines of England, work that now took a month could be done in three days. As winter approached the water would freeze and stop the water-wheel, thereby depriving the men of all but manual power. Working with such totally inadequate equipment it took them until the summer of 1864 to strike any gravel-bearing gold. With a steam engine, iron pumps and hydraulic hoses, the expedition might well have been more rewarding. Its members worked on the site for over a year and a half; they recovered $450 worth of gold and spent $26,000. Still, Evans' faith in the country never faltered. "The country is teeming with wealth," he said, "but more than four times the time and expense is lost in coping with difficulties with inadequate machinery."

A very different story can be told of the Billy Barker Company. Billy Barker was a seaman and a world-wide wanderer who arrived in Victoria (in reduced circumstances and a troublesome mood) in 1858. He became entangled in a saloon brawl and was hauled up before the magistrate and rebuked. There is no doubt that he tried his luck on the Fraser bars in 1859. Three years later he turned up on Williams Creek and associated himself with six other Englishmen. They formed a company and started to sink a shaft below the canyon where the town of Barkerville now stands. The other miners ridiculed them, as until then all the gold had been found in comparatively shallow diggings above the canyon. Billy Barker and his associates were down to 35 feet when the money ran out. Judge Begbie loaned them $700 (whether it was government money or from his private purse is not clear) with the idea of helping them get out of the country. Instead they sank their shaft another 17 feet and struck a pocket of nuggets. In the saloons of Richfield and Antler Town Billy Barker and his friends went on such a spree that Bishop Hills of Victoria, who was visiting the Cariboo at the time, noted it disapprovingly in his diary. Charles Hankin, the company secretary, seemed to be a more responsible type and arranged the working of the claim so well that (according to reports) $600,000 worth of gold was recovered.

Then the rush started and the whole area above the canyon was prospected and staked. Out of this developed such famous claims as "Cariboo" Cameron's at Camerontown. Billy Barker went down to Victoria, married a widow newly arrived from England, and returned with his bride to the Cariboo. In a few months his wife left him for more congenial surroundings. Barker, always a free spender, continued to part with his money, grubstaking many a

The prime mover of the Cariboo mines. A Cornish water wheel and pump, Quesnel.

prospector to work hopeless claims. Eventually broke, he returned to prospecting himself for two or three years with no luck and then took a job as cook in a road construction camp. He drifted down to Victoria, penniless and ill, and died in the Old Men's Home of that city on July 11, 1894.

WESTERN MINER

Miners at Windlass, Bill Barker's claim, Williams Creek about 1863.

John "Cariboo" Cameron, with Robert Stevenson and two others, late in the fall of 1862 found the famous Cameron claim about a mile down the creek from Barker's. They sank a shaft and took out a small quantity of gold, then left to winter in Victoria. During that winter Cameron bought out two of his partners; he came back in the spring and in four months took out close to $250,000 in gold. He left the Cariboo that fall to return to his home in Ontario's Glengarry County, where he bought a farm and invested in industrial and mining ventures in central Canada. These proved ill-founded and he returned to die in the Cariboo in 1888 — as poor as when he first arrived.

B.C. MINISTRY OF MINES

The ruins of "Cariboo Cameron's" cabin at Barkerville, as they appeared in 1902.

Changes were not slow in coming. The shallow diggings that had made a few individuals rich without much outlay of capital were being superseded by shafts driven 50 or 60 feet below the surface to bedrock. These entailed a greater degree of uncertainty, much more work, and a longer wait before any gold surfaced. A claim now could not be worked by one or two miners in a loose partnership, but required the steady work of a dozen or more individuals with different skills banded together in some more structured organization. The task called for managerial skills and somebody with access to enough money to pay for supplies and living expenses until the gold could be found and brought up. Thus the Cariboo mines changed very quickly from a field favoring the poor man to one that gave the greatest advantages to the man with capital. Miners banded together to work for wages, or to form commercial companies headed by men who possessed some capital. Thus we find that the major claims were now being worked by such outfits as the Diller Co., the Never Sweat Co., and the Grier Co. These claims were worked by crews of 20 or 30 men at wages ranging from $10 to $16 per day.

Entrance to the tunnel of the Neversweat mine, Williams Creek, about 1863.

The abandoned site of "Cariboo Cameron's" claim on Williams Creek. Many attempts have been made in past years to find the original source of the extreme richness of this claim.

Mining became a corporate business with all the essential auxiliary services. Three settlements took shape in Williams Creek: Richfield above the canyon with its government offices, Barkerville below the canyon with its saloons and dance halls, and Camerontown — where "Cariboo" Cameron had struck it so rich. All three in the days of the Cariboo Gold Rush were lively, bustling places. Along the narrow street next to the creek, miners' cabins jostled against the banks — the Bank of British North America, the Bank of British Columbia and the private one of Macdonald's — butchers' and blacksmiths' shops, eating places, the express company's office, the dance halls and saloons. Barkerville had a theatre and Richfield a hospital. The character of the population was changing: more British and Canadian and less American. Here could be found the sons of wealthy families in England, and magistrates and lawyers and others who had held good positions at home and for various reasons had lost them. Many were woefully unfitted for the task that they had come to perform, many on the verge of starvation. Some had adapted well and were a credit to their nationality and upbringing. These were in the mind of Judge Begbie when he wrote that it seemed "as though every good family of the east and of Great Britain had sent the best son they possessed for the development of the gold mines of Cariboo."

One of the vital services in the new goldfields was some institution where the miners could turn to sell their gold. The lure of gold prompted a group of merchants and bankers in the city of London to organize the Bank of British Columbia in 1862. Its first office in the Cariboo opened in the summer of 1863 at Richfield, mainly to buy gold from the miners on some 20 creeks in the neighborhood. The fineness of the gold and thus its value varied considerably from creek to creek, from a low of $14 an ounce for gold from a minor creek to a high of $19.25 for gold recovered from Lowhee, the best in the district. Bank staff had to exercise considerable judgment as mistakes could be costly. There was no assay office in the Cariboo for several years, and if a technical opinion was wanted the sample had to be sent to New Westminster — a round trip of some six to eight weeks.

Sluicing on Grouse Creek, Cariboo district, 1868. The Ne'er-do-well claim.

Partners at the head of the mine shaft, Sheepshead claim, Williams Creek, 1867.

Transportation of the gold was also a problem. The colonial government had tried to provide an armed escort to accompany the gold pack-trains going down to Yale, but this proved too costly. James Walker, general manager of the bank, arranged with Barnard's Express to send gold down three times a month with at least three guards. It was conveyed in burglar-proof safes built into the express wagons and guarded by two expressmen and a bank messenger. The combination of the locks were known only to the agent at the terminus and not to the drivers.

The expressmen had followed the miners wherever they went — by foot, by horse or mule, by steamer, and (when the roads were completed) by stage coach. Their services were prompt, efficient and regular. In lonely ravines, in the isolated claims on uncharted creeks, the agents of the express companies would come and pick up letters and gold, and leave any incoming mail or essential supplies. They knew where to go and what to do. The miners trusted

Some of the original rock work on the Cariboo wagon road through the Fraser canyon.

B.C. GOVERNMENT

Rock work which supported the Cariboo wagon road, built under supervision of the Royal Engineers in 1861-62, and still in use. Located a few miles north of Yale.

them to the limit and preferred to give their gold to them rather than the banks or the government gold escort. The express companies carried huge quantities, often worth as much as $100,000 per trip.

But before the express companies could operate to full capacity, roads had to be made. Immigrants to the Cariboo were continually protesting against high prices for food and shelter. Even those who could afford to stake and work a claim could seldom bring in adequate supplies or machinery for the job. In the deeper diggings they could not find enough help because nobody would work for a wage that failed to provide the bare necessities of life. A livable wage, from $10 to $14 a day, was more than any but the richest claims could stand. With freight at $1,200 per ton none but the most primitive tools could be imported. Without adequate communications the building up of mining communities and the development of the mines would be impossible.

Governor Douglas quickly realized the importance of communications in opening up the goldfields. It was through his endeavors that U.S. steamers were running up the Fraser to the head of navigation at Yale or Douglas. Thanks to him, miners had hacked out trails of uncertain workmanship and hasty construction from the head of Harrison Lake to Lillooet on the upper Fraser, and a trail had been built in the Fraser canyon from Yale to Spuzzum. The heavy rush of gold-seekers to the upper country in the spring and summer of 1860 put an intolerable strain on these slender means of access. The logical step was to improve the Douglas-Lillooet route. As mentioned in Chapter 1, the Royal Engineers were put to work on the southern section while J.W. Trutch, a civilian contractor, widened the middle and northern parts. Boats built in Victoria were put on the lakes and by the end of the mining season of 1862 the entire route could accommodate horses and wagons. In the upper country G.R. Wright was breaking a road through Clinton to the steamboat landing at Soda Creek. The great discoveries around Williams and other Cariboo creeks in 1862 attracted an increasing number of miners and businessmen. The enlarged Douglas-Lillooet route, taxed to capacity, could not bring up adequate amounts of provisions and supplies. Freight costs to the Cariboo were still too high, and so were prices. Better access to the gold country was urgently required.

By May of 1861, Governor Douglas had decided to undertake the greatest road-building project in British Columbia until the advent of Phil Gaglardi and the W.A.C. Bennett government of the 1960s. The famous Cariboo road began at Yale, the head of steam navigation. The seven miles to Sailors Bar was built by the Royal Engineers — a major job, entailing very heavy blasting, wall building, and side cutting. The eight miles from Sailors Bar to the crossing of the Fraser at the suspension bridge was built by Thomas Spence at a contract price of $36,000, with heavy blasting and much timbering. The Alexandra wire suspension bridge, built by J.W. Trutch, was an engineering landmark in the West. It was supported by two cables attached to towers erected on opposite sides of the river 285 feet apart and carrying a roadway 90 feet above the low water mark. The towers were of heavy wooden construction strengthened and held together by wrought-iron bolts. Carrying capacity was three tons but in 1871, when the expressman Barnard put on traction engines — the famous Thompson's Road Steamers — the bridge had to be strengthened. It was built as a private speculative venture under a five-year charter granted by the government to J.W. Trutch with permission to charge tolls: half a cent per pound on all goods and a smaller charge on animals and carriages. For more than 50 years it was in constant use until replaced by a stronger one of similar design.

The second Alexandra bridge at Spuzzum, built on lines similar to the original.

The original Alexandra toll bridge on the Cariboo wagon road, as built by civil engineer Joseph William Trutch.

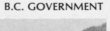

The present magnificent expressway Alexandra bridge, with the second still standing in the background.

The eleven-mile section on the other side of the river from the suspension bridge to Boston Bar was built under contract by J.W. Trutch. The 32 miles from Boston Bar to Lytton was built by Thomas Spence at a cost of $104,000. From Lytton to Spence's Ferry on the Thompson, a distance of 24 miles, was built by Walter Moberly, another famous B.C. road builder and engineer. Here the Thompson was crossed by a wooden bridge erected in 1864 by Thomas Spence. The route then struck north to Clinton to join Wright's road to Soda Creek and the steamboat landing. The magnitude of the work and the splendor of the scenery were described by a traveller of the time who wrote:

> From Yale to Boston Bar the road following the course of the Fraser through a canyon of surpassing grandeur has been either blasted out of granite bluffs almost sheer up from the river or formed by a wooden gallery or viaduct leading along the face of these bluffs and spanning the ravines which intersect it or built up of the masses of rock which have become detached from the cliffs above a rough slope at their base. This portion of the road is most solid and macadamized.

Even by the standards of today's road building it ranks as no mean achievement. By the standards of those days it was a source of wonder to all who travelled it. To the British Columbians of several generations it was an object of pride and a symbol of the romance attached to that far country known as the Cariboo.

B.C. GOVERNMENT

Spence's Bridge, where in 1864 Thomas Spence erected a wooden bridge which provided the last link in a continuous wagon road from Yale to Barkerville.

By 1864 the wagon road had been completed between Soda Creek and Quesnel and then east to Richfield and Camerontown, giving a continuous roadway for wheeled traffic the full distance of 370 miles from Yale to the center of the goldfields at Williams Creek.

But the economic impact of this continuous road on the mines of the Cariboo came just a year or so too late. By 1864 all the major discoveries had been made. There was great distress amongst miners and prospectors who could not find employment and amongst owners with little capital. The richer company mines such as the Caledonia Co. or the Artesian Gold Co. of Williams Creek were carrying on. All mine owners, though, were feeling the lack of steam power, of factory-made pumps and other machinery needed for practical work at deeper levels, especially in winter.

This challenge was taken up by some leading business people in the colony and in London. For a number of years, engineering circles in England had been interested in the application of the steam locomotive to road transportation. John Fowler, a Leeds manufacturer and an inventor in his own right, had perfected a mobile traction-type steam engine to be used in plowing; it was only one more step to adapt such an engine to hauling a train of wagons on the roads. By 1864 John Fowler & Co. were building traction engines for road use. J.W. Trutch and Janion, Green & Rhodes (Victoria merchants in the Cariboo) asked Fowler & Co. to consider sending some of their machines to work on the Cariboo road. Trutch was in England at the time; with Col. R.C. Moody of the Royal Engineers, he attended a demonstration by Fowler & Co. of one of their machines.

Both men were enthusiastic when they saw that the engines could draw loads of up to 12 tons at a rate of six or seven miles an hour, a load much heavier than any being hauled by horses or wagons then travelling the Cariboo road. The upshot was that the British Columbia Steam Traction Co. was formed to buy some of these machines and place them "for the conveyance of freight on the Waggon Roads of this Colony." Plans included the importation of 23 engines of 10 horse-power costing a manufacturer's price of £450 each, plus fifty wagons at £50 each. Forty men supplied by Fowler would be sent out from England to drive and service them. Each engine would draw two freight wagons loaded with six tons of merchandise and have a crew of three: a driver, his assistant, and a brakeman. It would burn wood and be supplied by depots spaced along the road.

The promoters approached the colonial government for concessions and permission to use the roads. They had been convinced by their research, according to their petition, "that these Machines are exactly adapted to perform the services which would be required of them in British Columbia and that by employing them the cost of transporting freight into the interior of the Country would be at once materially reduced." Permission was granted on March 10, 1864. But by the time the machines were to be shipped in the spring or summer of 1865, the mines were beginning to show signs of exhaustion; people were leaving the Cariboo for other goldfields. Freight was on the decline and the transportation business no longer looked so bright. Also, somebody must have taken a second look at the roads, for the bridges were not built to take 16-ton loads and would have had to be strengthened. The proposal was scrapped and no machines were sent out. Still, it is of interest that such ideas continued to be talked about and were finally put into practice six years later.

Alfred Waddington, one of the leading merchants of Victoria, had interests of his own in transportation problems of the Cariboo mines. He was the champion of what was hoped to be a new and shorter route to the Cariboo by way of Bute Inlet and Homathko River. This route began miles up the coast from New Westminster and the Fraser and thus (a strong point for Victorians) would not come within the trading area of that city. Unfortunately it traversed virtually unknown regions where nobody had been able to find a practical way over the coast mountains into the interior. Waddington was not discouraged. He obtained a franchise and a liberal grant of land from the colonial government to make a wagon road over the Bute-Homathko route. His powerful backers in London were also interested in steam transportation, as shown by his letter of August 29, 1867, to A.N. Birch, the Colonial Secretary: "A railway was the final objective of the parties with whom I am in negotiations. . . . It may be very possible that they might have to begin with a Traction engine road." The government seemed sympathetic to his ideas and he left for England in October of that year. His backers in London had retained the services of Thomas Brassey, a leading British railway contractor and the builder of the Grand Trunk Railway of Canada. They took the project very seriously and all that held them back were the Indian troubles that Waddington's men had encountered in the building of a section of the road and the uncertainties of the Cariboo mining scene. Nothing material seems to have come of these discussions but the idea of using steam on the roads of B.C. persisted.

It fell to Francis Jones Barnard, the pioneer Cariboo expressman, to put the idea to a practical test. His career was intimately connected with both the Fraser River and Cariboo gold rushes. He came to B.C. with a party of gold-seekers in 1859. At the height of the excitement he arrived at Yale where he staked a claim. He then sold out and took a position there as town constable. This did not last for long and he is next found as purser on the steamer *Yale*, built by the citizens of that town in hope of breaking the steamship monopoly on the Fraser. Unfortunately the *Yale* blew herself to pieces in a boiler explosion some two miles above Hope. The captain and four others were killed but Barnard was thrown into the river by the blast and survived. He started a one-man express business in the autumn of 1860, travelling over the trail just completed from Yale to Lytton through the canyon.

As the center of mining moved northward Barnard followed, making the long round trip of more than 750 miles from Yale to the Cariboo creeks on foot — a journey probably never equalled by any other expressman. In time he was able to acquire pack animals, then light wagons or dog-carts, over certain sections of the way. In May 1864, when the Cariboo wagon road was completed, he put on a line of 14 passenger four-horse stage coaches to run twice a week between Yale and Soda Creek. When the wagon road finally reached Williams Creek in 1865 he began to run regular stages into Barkerville. A journey which had taken three to four weeks only five years earlier was accomplished in comparative comfort in a matter of four days.

Cariboo Waggon Road

In 1865 Barnard's stages carried 1500 passengers to and from the Cariboo and brought down $4,600,000 worth of gold. Barnard was aware of efforts to bring mechanical traction to the roads of B.C. He was also aware of the many difficulties. He thought he might overcome these with a new type of a traction engine designed in Edinburgh by R.W. Thompson and built by Tennant & Co. of Leith. The engines were some four tons lighter than those built by John Fowler of Leeds and had a novel feature — solid india rubber tires attached to the wheels. It was claimed that the tires acted as excellent springs, easing wear and tear on the engine and enabling

43

it to run on the roads at a sensible speed. They were perfectly noiseless and could be run without injury to any well-made road, a great selling point with government officials. Barnard ordered several, including two that were custom-made for Cariboo passengers, mail and express. The engines were mounted on three wheels, two at the rear for driving and the front one, much smaller, for steering. Each engine would haul specially constructed passenger coaches and freight wagons. "Steam to Cariboo," trumpeted the *Victoria Colonist*. "The British Columbia General Transportation Company will place four of Thompson's Patent Road Steamers on the route between Yale and Barkerville in the First Week of April."

But the very first train from Yale in early April got stuck one-third of the way to its destination. Another stalled on Jackass Mountain, a victim of rough winding mountain roads made slippery by the spring breakup. The mud would spurt from under the wheels between the india rubber and the iron rim. Thus lubricated, only the rim would revolve and the machines became stalled. Barnard promptly shipped the machines he had not paid for back to Scotland. The one that he owned was sold to Jeremiah Rogers for logging operations on English Bay. That was the end of one of the more imaginative efforts to solve the transportation problems of the Cariboo mines. For the next 40 years the only way to get freight in and out was by horsedrawn stage or wagon.

B.C. GOVERNMENT

How the public and the mails travelled in the early days of mining in B.C. An old time stage coach.

Another bizarre innovation designed to increase the capacity of the animal pack-train was the importation of 21 Manchurian camels by Frank Laumeister, a New Westminster packer. One camel could carry twice the load of a mule, and it had no feeding problems. (The first 100 miles from Yale and the last 70 miles into the Cariboo offered little or no grass at any time of year, and grains had to be hauled in to feed the livestock as it passed. Camels, carrying their own food internally, could pass through these regions without trouble.) The exotic beasts were first tried on the Douglas-Lillooet portages and proved partially successful. As freight declined on this route with the opening of the wagon road through the Fraser canyon, they were moved to Quesnel to work the 60-mile stretch into Barkerville, where their splay feet were expected to prevent them from sinking into the holes made in the road by the iron hooves of passing pack-train mules and horses. But the camels' feet sank into these water-logged holes and were spread out there by the weight of the heavy loads, sticking them fast in the middle of the road. Much time and effort went into getting them out again. All the other animals on the road became frightened by the peculiar odor of the sweating camels and would stampede off the road and ruin their bundles. After several mishaps like this the other packers took the matter to the courts and by court injunction the camels were ordered off the road. Eventually they were turned loose — and for many years animals and travellers would be frightened by the unexpected appearance of one of these outcasts.

Where the Royal Engineers achieved their greatest triumph. The Fraser canyon as it appears today. Instead of the narrow gravel Cariboo wagon road, the magnificent two-lane Trans-Canada motor expressway.

B.C. GOVERNMENT

The prosperity of the mines depended upon the carrying business. It lay in the hands of a few individuals, often operating on capital borrowed from the banks at a high rate of interest. It was also highly seasonal as packing could be undertaken to the upper country during no more than seven months in the year. From November to March all teams were taken off the roads to graze in the lower country. Most of the packers were connected in some way with the merchants of Victoria or New Westminster. Because of tight groupings of established packers and traders, newcomers would be unable to handle deliveries to the mines. So the sponsors of the British Columbia Steam Traction Engine Co. had good grounds for optimism in their prospectus of 1864.

> It is confidently anticipated (they wrote) that the substitution of steam power for oxen and mules in hauling freight along the roads will occasion quite a revolution in the business prospects on the Capital invested in carrying out the enterprise.

The industry not only required such conventional services as food, shelter, and retail stores for its workers, but also several special ones not required by other enterprises: a mint, assaying offices, and banks. To keep the gold within the country the government recognized that these services must be provided. Writing to the Secretary of State for the Colonies, Governor Douglas had pointed out:

> Much anxiety has been expressed by the miners generally upon the subject of banks of deposit which are greatly needed in every district of British Columbia, the miners' only alternative at present being to bury his gold dust for security . . . but were banks of deposit established they would willingly pay a monthly percentage of any sums they might deposit.

B.C. GOVERNMENT

The Gold Commissioner's office, Barkerville.

46

A Barkerville saloon of the 1860's, showing gold dust scales. Barkerville Historical Park.

By the time the Cariboo gold boom peaked there were six firms engaged in the storage or purchase of gold dust and bars: Wells Fargo & Co., Marchand & Co., Robertson & Co. (assayers), and three banks (the private bankers Macdonald & Co., the Bank of British North America and the Bank of British Columbia). All six had offices in Victoria while the banks had further branches in the Cariboo.

It was partly the insistence of the manager of the Bank of British Columbia, J.D. Walker, that led to the reactivation of the gold escort in 1863. The gold escort was an institution that the government hoped would provide safe transportation for the miners' gold to the coast. It was first tried out in 1861 and provided much of the drama associated with gold-rush days. Well mounted, heavily armed and smartly uniformed, the escort surrounding the gold-carrying cart presented a picture of affluence and wellbeing seen nowhere else in the colony. Financially it was a disaster — the miners did not trust it and neither did some of the banks. The manager of Macdonald's branch at Williams Creek flatly refused to use its services; like most of the miners, he put his faith in the integrity, efficiency and speed of the expressmen. Through lack of business the gold escort was discontinued in 1863, never to be reinstated. The banks also were put to considerable disadvantage through the enacting of the Gold Export Tax in 1864. This was an attempt by the government to recover some of the monies spent on making the roads to the mines, by levying a duty of two shillings per ounce on any gold handed into a bank for deposit or transshipments. The miners found it more profitable to take gold out of the country on their person and sell it to the U.S. mint at San Francisco.

Assaying was another problem that found no satisfactory solution

47

until the mines went on the decline. The gold found in each creek differed markedly in fineness and quality. It was said that an experienced miner could tell the source by handling a sample. This would lift the wraps from many a discovery in a minor creek. A prospector would turn up at a bank in Richfield or Barkerville with a bag of gold dust and say that it came from Williams Creek or Antler or some other well-known location, but the bank manager would examine it and say it came from somewhere else. The word would get around and the prospector would be followed when he left town. In 1864 the Bank of British Columbia put an assayer to work in the bank office; by the time the government was persuaded to open an assay office the peak had passed and the mines were being abandoned.

One of the more colorful episodes of the gold-rush days concerned the founding of the mint at New Westminster. British Columbia from the beginning had suffered from the lack of a circulating medium for ordinary commercial transactions. Gold in its natural state could not perform this function, and the merchants feared that much business was being lost through miners' taking their gold out of the country and having it changed into coin in San Francisco. They petitioned the government for action. The first attempt to solve the problem was the establishment of a government assay office in New Westminster, to place on gold a more accurate value that would be recognized by all the merchants in the colony. Still, this was not as convenient as converting the gold into coin, so the public (through the newspapers) agitated for the establishment of a mint. At last the pressure grew so strong that Governor Douglas authorized Captain W.D. Gosset, the Colonial Treasurer, to buy machinery and set up a branch of the assay office to mint coins.

Authority came in the form of a letter written under instructions by the Colonial Secretary on November 14, 1861. "I am instructed by His Excellency," it read, "to authorize you to dispatch Mr. Claudet to San Francisco to obtain the necessary machinery for coining at the Assay Office in New Westminster pieces of the value of Twenty and Ten Dollars American currency." The machinery was made by the Vulcan Foundry of San Francisco and arrived at Esquimalt on March 2, 1862. It reached New Westminster aboard *H.M.S. Forward* in April. Captain Gosset lost no time in setting it up in a building on Columbia Street, specially built for the purpose. Douglas had second thoughts and told Gosset (much to his disgust) to await events and put the machinery in storage. Eventually a few gold coins of the ten and twenty dollars were struck and became collectors' items. There the matter lay. No coins ever reached the public, and the government and merchants continued to import coins from abroad. The banks issued banknotes for public circulation which proved more acceptable than gold coins.

The early period of gold mining in the Cariboo was drawing to a close. Surface diggings had become depleted. Shafts had been sunk to try and reach the bedrock where the nuggets could be found hidden in the rock crevices. But high prices and the uncertainties of finding such gold had reduced the number of claims being worked. Then there was the inability of the homemade pumps to cope with the underground water which filled up the shafts. It has been said that $1,000,000 was spent on Williams Creek in efforts to drain out the water. Lightning Creek below Van Winkle had become deserted because of this problem. Other discoveries in British Columbia — the Stikine River in 1862, the Kootenays and Leech River on Vancouver Island in 1864, the Big Bend excitement of 1866, and the Peace-Omineca of 1869 — drew away hundreds from the Cariboo.

"Mining," wrote Alexander Allan, publisher of the *Cariboo Sentinel*, "is unlike any other legitimate occupation or business — it is so uncertain. It is simply a game of chance." His paper at last had to admit in 1868 that there was "a present depression" with "dull times" ahead. The situation was not static; a few new gold-bearing creeks were found and there were some new finds on the old ones. Antler Creek had been practically abandoned to all but the Chinese since 1863. Lowhee had only 150 men working in 1865 and was as good as closed in 1871. Lightning, almost deserted in 1868, had a brief comeback and by 1874 was producing more than Williams Creek, but then it went into another sharp decline. Grouse and Mosquito creeks followed the same pattern as the majority of Cariboo creeks; early discoveries, brief workings, then abandonment and new discoveries and the same cycle over again. The early period can be said to have ended around 1876. In that year on Williams Creek there were 27 companies working compared with 169 in 1862 and an undetermined greater number in 1863.

B.C. MINISTRY OF MINES

Gold dredge on the Fraser at Lillooet, 1899.

49

The impact of the Cariboo gold rush upon the future of British Columbia was immense. Its men and events laid the foundations upon which this province has been built. Although thousands left, many stayed to become wealthy by other means. Cattle ranching, started to satisfy the demands of the Cariboo miners, became an established industry. James Laidlaw, a successful Cariboo miner, stayed to put his money to work in the first salmon cannery erected in this province. Some, like "Cariboo" Cameron's partner, Robert Stevenson, invested in Chilliwack real estate. Others, like Tom Cunningham of New Westminster, founded retail and wholesale establishments in the cities. Many became prosperous farmers, or industrialists like R.H. Alexander, manager of Hastings Sawmill. Contributions to the welfare of the province were made by hundreds less fortunate who travelled the road to the Cariboo — people such as John Evans, who stayed to become a respected citizen there and a member of the provincial legislature, or Harry Jones, a member of the Evans party, and an M.L.A. for two terms, who ran through two fortunes and died in 1936 at the great age of 97, still in the Cariboo.

The gateway to the Cariboo gold fields. Quesnel, as it appears today.   B.C. GOVERNMENT

A plaque commemorating the technical work of the Royal Engineers in surveying, locating and building the wagon roads in B.C. so that miners could carry on their work.

The country where, 100 years ago, prospectors roamed in search of gold. The British Columbia-Alaska border, with the great glacier in the background.

3

Gold : North ~ South East ~ West

Nine hundred miles north, by sailing boat from Victoria, near the little Russian-Alaskan town of Wrangell, lies the mouth of the Stikine River. The existence of gold along the river had been known to the Hudson's Bay Company employees there before the 1860's, but it was up to a French-Canadian named Alexander Choquette to bring this to the attention of the public.

Choquette left Victoria in May 1861 for the Stikine River in an Indian canoe. That summer he worked the bars of the river some 100 miles from its mouth. When he returned in the autumn with gold, the *Colonist* reports attracted the attention of many miners wintering in Victoria; the spring of 1862 saw a small fleet of vessels leaving Victoria almost weekly for the north. Advertisements offering passage to the mouth of the Stikine filled the Victoria papers. A minor rush was in the making. Choquette and eight other French-Canadians left Victoria on January 27 on the schooner *Kingfisher*. By May about 200 miners were at the mouth of the Stikine. As soon as the ice cleared they ascended the river and began to work the bars.

The experience of one miner was typical. He arrived at Buck's Bar on May 22, and with four others began working a bar on the south side of the river — until the water rose three days later and drove them out. The paydirt was from six to twenty inches thick and they were making from $300 to $400 per day. The party then moved to another bar three miles further up the river where the story was repeated. The spring freshet drove them out, but they left the diggings for the south on July 1 with a nice pile.

The center of mining was at the head of navigation at a place still called Glenora, which then consisted of half-a-dozen log cabins built on a flat. Facilities for transportation sprang up with the speed that marked most gold rushes. The Hudson's Bay Company put its new steamer *Labouchere* into service to convey passengers and freight from Victoria to Wrangell. Up the Stikine plied a small sternwheeler — the *Flying Dutchman* — and in June "Barnett's Stickeen River Express" began regular runs. After the level of the water had fallen in July mining began again. Some bars paid as much as $800 per man per day but these were exceptions. Most paid only a dollar or two for a day's work. Prospectors travelled through the Great Canyon and into the upper reaches of the river, but with so little success that in August about 200 of them returned in dismay to Victoria. Another 80 decided to stick out the winter of 1862-63 in log cabins around Glenora. Findings were spotty in the spring and the workings were shallow, so the field became virtually abandoned by the winter of 1863.

One of the more remarkable aspects of this minor rush lay in its international implications. To get to the goldfield all miners and their supplies had to pass through Russian territory. The Russian American Company controlled the mouth of the Stikine River and it was only through the good offices of the Hudson's Bay Company and its close working agreement over so many years with the Russian traders that the miners were able to proceed up the river without hindrance. The Russian American Company was in no position to handle a rush of individualistic and in many cases lawless miners; it was delighted to let the Hudson's Bay Company handle the arrangements.

When the miners did arrive in the interior they found an unexplored and unorganized territory without as much as a Hudson's Bay Company fort or official. For seven months in 1862 between 300 and 500 miners and prospectors lived at peace under no recognized constitutional or Company authority without a single reported act of violence. The relationship between them and the Indians remained good.

In the fall of 1862 the British authorities in Whitehall organized the northern section of British Columbia into a colony under the name of "Stickin." Governor Douglas of British Columbia was named administrator and British law was proclaimed under the jurisdiction of the B.C. Supreme Court. When the shallow claims were worked out the Stikine country returned to the fur trade until the Cassier discoveries of 1872 opened up the interior again.

Reports had been circulating in Victoria in 1860 that gold had been discovered in the Peace River. According to the *Colonist*, a party of miners had found gold prospects on the Peace "three hundred miles further north of Alexandra." In 1861 William Cust and Edward Cary followed the old fur traders' route from Alexandria via the Fraser, Nechako, and Stuart rivers to Fort McLeod. They drifted 200 miles by canoe downstream on the Peace to the Grand Canyon. There they obtained about $1,000 worth of gold and in

September retraced their steps to the Fraser. In 1862 a party of 25 came up the same way from Alexandria, worked the bars up to Findlay Forks, and ascended the Findlay River. At the end of the season they returned to Quesnel, but some other parties wintered on the Findlay River. That was the year that firmly established the presence of gold in the Peace country. More than 150 miners visited the Peace in 1863, with 70 from the Cariboo in April, May and June. 'Twelve-Foot' Davis, a noted prospector and fur trader, navigated the Fraser and connecting waterways from its mouth to Fort St. James in two ten-ton boats with supplies. The returns in 1863 from the Peace were very poor and only a few remained. They would trap in winter, engage in fur-trading with the Indians, and do a little prospecting each summer. For the next few years nothing really caught the imagination of the public until the 1869 discovery on Vital Creek in the Omineca district.

The Omineca gold rush of 1869-70 stems largely from the reports of the Peace River Prospecting Party. This party occupies a unique niche in the annals of gold mining in B.C. It was supported by the public and partially funded by the Colonial government. Business in British Columbia at this time was going through a depression. The surface placer mines of the Cariboo had become exhausted;

B.C. GOVERNMENT

The Big Bend rush of 1865-66. Downie Creek, in the heart of the Rockies.

the fields in the Kootenays and in the Big Bend had proved disappointing. Both the public and the businessmen felt that new gold fields had to be found. At a meeting of Cariboo citizens at Quesnel, G.B. Wright (the great roadbuilder) and Edgar Dewdney (later Lieutenant-Governor) were chosen to raise funds and arrange to send out a prospecting party to the north. The appeal for funds was successful with over $1200 being raised. The committee persuaded the government at Victoria to give $1000 and the Peace River Prospecting Party was born.

Michael Byrnes, a former scout for the Collins Overland Telegraph line, was selected as leader and Vital La Force (another former scout) joined the expedition as a private member. The success of the party lay largely in the hands of these two men, both experts in wilderness travel. They had explored the Nass, Skeena, and Stikine valleys in the years 1865-67 for the telegraph company. As the overland telegraph project had now collapsed they were unemployed. Their new employers, the citizens of the Cariboo, issued precise instructions to Michael Byrnes as leader. "You will try," wrote the committee, "as far as your judgement allows, the various streams forming the Finlay's Branch and not diverge too near the coast or too far to the east as the Peace River has already been prospected."

The party struck eastward from Takla Lake. They made their first find and named it Vital Creek. The claims were worked all that summer and in the fall Byrnes returned to Quesnel. Other returning parties agreed that the diggings were shallow, limited in extent, and nowhere very rich. But because of the variety of rumors circulating, the public was led to believe in the extravagant richness of the find. Many thought that the members of the Byrnes party were holding back vital information gained with public funds in order to exploit the field to their own advantage after the spring break-up of 1870. The newspapers were by no means helpful, publishing contradictory reports that left the public excited and suspicious. This all laid the groundwork for an early spring rush.

The rush started early, in the depth of a Cariboo winter. R.J. Lamont was running the "Omineca Express" from Quesnel to Vital Creek, by dog-train and toboggan. He started from Quesnel in January 1870 and experienced a hard journey to the creek; on the return trip he had his hands and face frozen. In the spring and summer of 1870 the service became a regular one. By the spring thaw 150 white miners and about 100 Chinese were on their way from Quesnel to the Omineca. About the same time 50 men travelled to the mines via the Skeena. In all, at the height of the mining season in July, there were about 350 miners on the creek. Victoria held great hopes about the richness of the field. "We have lately received very good accounts from Peace River," wrote Philip J. Hankin, Colonial Secretary at Victoria, to the Duke of Buckingham on March 11, 1870, "and many say it is likely to prove even richer than the Cariboo."

Although a few of the diggings proved profitable, most of the miners became discouraged and left — but not the Germansen party that found gold 50 miles east in Germansen Creek. When Germansen and his group returned to Vital Creek in the third week of August they sparked a rush. Many set off that night and picked their way by lighted candles held in broken bottles. By the next evening Vital camp was almost deserted — the whole population was busily staking claims on the new creek before freeze-up.

The spring of 1871 saw the real rush begin to the Omineca mines.

Sternwheelers began to run from Cottonwood Canyon to Fort George and at times even up to Giscome Portage. The summer of that year offered one of the most amazing feats of steamboating that ever took place on B.C. waterways. G.R. Wright's sternwheeler *Enterprise*, which had plied for eight years between Soda Creek and Quesnel, was taken off to run up to the Omineca mines. She navigated the canyons below Fort George with the assistance of her passengers and ascended Nechako River, finally arriving on Takla Lake — a feat that no other sternwheeler ever accomplished. Unfortunately the project was not a financial success and she was abandoned on Trembleur Lake, where for many years her hulk could be seen on the lakeshore. The creek itself was not rich and the miners drifted to Manson Creek, eight miles to the south, or departed broke. Their greatest number in the Omineca was about 600 in 1872. When good reports of mining in the Cassiar reached the camps in 1873 the crowd dwindled.

The country which witnessed the Omineca gold rush of 1871. Looking up the Omineca valley.

The discovery of gold in the Cassiar district (the name applied in the early days to the mining region in and about the Liard River basin) came through the explorations of an independent trapper-trader. The discovery is credited to Angus McCulloch and his partner Henry Thibert.

McCulloch was a trapper-prospector who had taken part in the Big Bend rush of 1865-66. Thibert, born in Montreal, lived in Minnesota for many years and in June 1870 outfitted there to pass two or three winters in the North West Territories. In the summer of 1871 with McCulloch he passed over the Rockies onto the Pacific side and in the spring of 1872 they followed the course of the Liard to Dease Lake. Here in the summer they struck promising findings. Thibert went into winter quarters at Buck's Bar near Glenora while

57

McCulloch pressed on to Victoria to try and interest the government in giving him some money for the coming mining season. He returned north in February of 1873 to rejoin Thibert but lost his way and froze to death in a snowstorm on the Stikine. Undismayed, Thibert went into partnership with several other French-Canadians wintering at Buck's Bar and trekked back again to Dease Lake. They found gold. As the news spread hundreds of miners poured in from Victoria and the depleted creeks in the Omineca.

The diggings around Dease Lake were much more accessible than the other minor goldfields. The route from Victoria was by coastal steamer up to Wrangell (U.S. territory by then) and from there by shallow draught riverboat up the Stikine River to Glenora. The remaining 85 miles could be made on a trail of sorts cut out by Captain William Moore terminating on Dease Lake. The field easily supported 1200 miners, more than any other secondary field in this period. Dease Creek was staked for almost its entire 16 miles, with so many wingdams exposing areas of its bed that the flow of water became blocked. Some of the older hands from the winter of 1873-74 started to mine before the spring break-up. They chopped ice out of the side of the creek bed, thawed out the sand and gravel with huge bonfires and then washed it in the rockers. Optimism soared in the field and at Victoria — the Cassiar mines would prove another Cariboo and help to solve the economic ills besetting the province.

The Stikine River valley, witness of much activity in the days of the Cassiar gold rush of 1874-75.

Panning for gold in a famous location. Miners on McDame Creek, Omineca district, in 1931.

That Dease Creek is very rich (wrote Gold Commissioner Sullivan from Dease Creek on June 13, 1874) is the opinion of everyone here at present. The Neil-McArthur Co. took out for five days work $2,700. Two men in another claim working with a rocker took out 50 oz. for one day's work. The miners who are able to work their ground have all obtained gold in paying quantities and some have realized handsome amounts.

New method of prospecting. A hydroplane at Dease Lake, northern British Columbia, 1925.

Another encouraging sign came in the summer of 1874 when Henry McDame discovered a rich find in the creek which took his name some 90 miles above Dease Lake. It yielded the largest nugget found in any B.C. goldfield up to that date. Alfred Freeman, while sluicing on the Discovery claim, cast aside a large boulder. When he made a closer inspection he was amazed to find it was a nugget weighing 73 ounces.

Some finds were made nearby, but nothing major. Deep-pit mining was started by four comparatively large companies without result. The Empire Co. finally abandoned its shaft at 1400 feet without striking bedrock. The White Grouse struck bedrock at 1580 feet but found no signs of gold. The decline of the field is shown by the drastic decline in wages within two years. In 1874 mechanics could command $20 a day, and laborers $15. Two years later, mechanics' wages were as low as $7.50 per day while laborers could command only $6. From the white miners' standpoint the field was worked out by 1880. The Cassiar district was not to be revitalized through minerals until the coming of asbestos mining in the 1950s.

In what is now southeastern British Columbia the goldrush phenomenon occurred early. It has been mentioned in Chapter 1 how the Hudson's Bay Company traders at Fort Colville had obtained gold

Hydraulic mining. The elevator and pipeline used in gold mining in the Cariboo in the 1880's and 1890's.

in trade from the Indians. In the days of the Fraser River gold excitement, two U.S. cavalrymen riding with dispatches encamped at Rock Creek — a small stream flowing into the Kettle River 14 miles west of Midway. They picked up a few nuggets from the creek bed and continued on their way to spread the word. By the fall of 1860 some hundreds of miners, mostly U.S., had gathered on the creek. A settlement grew up; to try and keep the trade within the colony and not allow it to go by default to the Americans, Governor Douglas commissioned Edgar Dewdney to build a trail from the head of steamboat navigation on the Fraser at Hope. This first section of southern trans-provincial highway known as the Dewdney Trail was built in the years 1860-61. As the shallower diggings became depleted the miners left, though the creek has intermittently been worked by various methods since that time: by individual placer mining, by hydraulicking (through the Laura Hydraulic Co. of Victoria from 1888-90) by dredging, and by shafting to bedrock.

Far more spectacular was the rush to Wild Horse Creek near Fort Steele in the Kootenays, some 50 miles north of the International Boundary, in 1863-64. Governor Frederick Seymour of British Columbia sent his colonial secretary, Arthur N. Birch, to report.

> We arrived at the mines (Secretary Birch wrote) on the 26th day from Hope. . . . I found about 700 men resident at the mines and I was informed that at least 300 were prospecting in the neighborhood. . . . At the time of my arrival, 50 Sluice Companies were at work employing from 5 to 25 men and taking out from $300 to $1,000 per diem. . .

> Seventy men were employed in constructing a large upper ditch some 5 miles in length which it was expected would be completed in the present month when more than 100 hill claims which were laying over for want of water would commence work. Laborers were receiving $7 per day. . . . A town of no inconsiderable size has already sprung up upon the creek — 4 restaurants are established. Numerous substantial stores have been erected. A large Brewery has also been established and had commenced working. The entire supplies are at present packed in from Lewiston, Walla-Walla, Walluld and Umatilla Landing in Washington Territory and the State of Oregon.

Governor Seymour, like governor Douglas four years earlier at Rock Creek, faced the problem of channeling the trade to New Westminster and B.C. merchants. The solution seemed to be to extend the Dewdney Trail to Wild Horse Creek and the Kootenays. This was accomplished in 1865 but by then the rush had peaked and the mines were on the decline. It was not until 35 years later and the coming of the Canadian Pacific Railway's Crow's Nest Branch that the trade of the Kootenays was finally wrested from the hands of the Americans.

By 1865 gold was beckoning from southeastern British Columbia, far up the Columbia River where it takes its big bend. The Big Bend rush also attracted more Americans than Canadians. As usual, rumor exaggerated the facts and in 1866 a small steamer edged its way up the Columbia from the Dalles in Washington Territory. Most miners kept to the banks of the Columbia but some went up Downie or Carne's creeks and brought out good takings. The Big Bend rush was short lived and over-subscribed. The U.S. boat made three more trips that summer and the colonial government contracted with Walter Moberly to build a trail from the east end of Shuswap Lake to the little settlement of La Porte near Downie Creek. But the gold was not there in paying quantities and it was all over by 1867.

Some ten miles northwest of Victoria in the Malahat district is Leech River. That was where Peter Leech, a former member of the Royal Engineers, discovered a stream with paydirt on July 14, 1864. At the peak of the ensuing rush some 400 miners were washing the gravel. A townsite was laid out for a new Barkerville — the Island's Governor, Arthur Kennedy, made an official visit in May 1865. But the diggings were shallow; though a number of bars produced well for a short time, the placer mines soon became depleted and the miners left with $100,000 or so. Today the mining community of Leechtown is no more and the wealth of the district lies in the forests and not in the ground.

From 1875 to 1900 there were no new goldfields in B.C. Until about 1880 gold annually produced the greatest wealth and employed (directly and indirectly) the largest number of people in the province. Then coal took over. In the nineties, silver and lead were the metals most in demand; early in the twentieth century, copper became king. Times have changed since 1880, when 292 of 373 mining companies working in B.C. were after gold. Of these, 205 were working by sluicing, 41 by hydraulicking, and 46 by tunnel and shaft; only 28 companies were engaged entirely in prospecting.

B.C. MINISTRY OF MINES

Cariboo Hydraulic Mining Company's operations on the south fork of the Quesnel River in 1897.

61

Up to that point all the gold recovered had been taken out of placers. No hard-rock mining for gold was being carried on, although some excellent ledges had been found. In hard-rock or quartz mining, hand drilling was used for most of the nineteenth century. Most common was the slow and arduous two-man method whereby one man swung a heavy sledge-hammer to drive home a chisel-shaped drill held by his partner. In the sixties, power drills run by compressed air were developed for railway tunneling but these did not come into general use by B.C.'s mining industry until the nineties. When ways were found to cool the bit as it bored through the rock by applying water or other cooling agents, mechanical drilling became commonplace in B.C. mines.

One of the first successful hard-rock gold mining operations in B.C. was Hedley's Nickel Plate Mine, 4000 feet above the town of Hedley in the Similkameen district of Southern B.C. Prospectors Francis Wollaston and Constantine Arundel found a rich outcrop of gold-bearing ore on Nickel Plate Mountain in the summer of 1898. In the fall of that year their surface samples at the Provincial Exhibition at New Westminster were noticed by M.K. Rodgers, an engineer employed by mining magnate Marcus Daly of Butte, Montana. Upon receipt of an on-the-spot report from the workings, Daly bought out the prospectors (reportedly for $60,000) and started to cut trails, erect a campsite and bring in supplies.

Marcus Daly

B.C. PROVINCIAL ARCHIVES

When Marcus Daly was principal owner: A group of office and executive employees of the Nickel Plate gold mine at Hedley, photographed July 14, 1907.

In its prosperous years— an ore train leaving the Nickel Plate gold mine head, Hedley, B.C.

WESTERN MINER

Permanent mining began in 1899. Enough ore was found by 1902 to justify the erection of a stamp mill, and the selected property at the foot of the mountain was given outright by a real estate developer at the tiny settlement of Hedley. With the exception of lumber, all machinery and supplies had to be brought 50 miles from Penticton by four-horse teams. There was no telephone and the telegraph office was at Vernon, two days travel time away. All 40 stamps of the mill started up in May or June 1904, and their muffled roar was a feature of the town for the next 50 years.

62

Every month two gold bricks came down to Penticton under special guard and were sent by Dominion Express to Seattle. Concentrates were sacked and hauled by horse-drawn wagon at $9 per ton to Penticton and from there by rail to the smelter at Tacoma. On the return journey the wagons would bring back supplies to Hedley at a contract rate of $20 per ton. The round trip usually took about a week.

After Marcus Daly's death and the failure of several attempts to locate new veins, the estate manager became very pessimistic. M.K. Rodgers, the engineer whose report had sparked the project, then interested the United States Steel Corporation in the property and a subsidiary (Exploration Syndicate No. 1) was instructed to make an examination and eventually an offer. For a purchase price of $715,000 U.S. Steel, under Rodgers, became the new owners. A new company, Hedley Gold Mining Co., took over and paid a substantial dividend for many years.

One of the reasons behind the purchase was the fact that the mine at last was getting adequate transportation. The Great Northern Railway in its bid for a southern trans-provincial line had authorized the building of trackage from Keremeos to Princeton by way of Hedley, and regular train service started on December 23, 1909. Three months earlier L.L. Merrill of U.S. Steel, president of Hedley Gold Mining, had arrived at Hedley from Spokane in the superintendent's private car.

WESTERN MINER

View of the stamp mill and cyanide plant of the Nickel Plate Mine at Hedley, B.C., 1913.

The period from 1910 to 1916 was one of the most properous in the mine's life. Rising labor costs closed it temporarily in 1921 and early 1922, but for the next eight years the mine and mill were in continuous operation. It closed for another two years in 1930 (after extracting some $13 million in gold), and fell into the hands of the Kelowna Exploration Company, who operated it from 1934 to 1956. The gradually increasing price for gold in the thirties helped its successful rehabilitation. In the summer of 1956 increasing production costs, depletion of the ore veins, and the fixed price of gold made it uneconomical to carry on and the mine was closed permanently.

60 years after: The abandoned site of the stamp mill and cyanide plant of the Nickel Plate gold mine at Hedley, B.C.

The most widely publicized of all gold rushes was that to the Klondike in 1898. The diggings were found on the Klondike River and its tributaries around Dawson in the Yukon, and therefore are not within the story of mining in B.C. But as the quickest and easiest way into the Yukon was by steamer up the B.C. coast, Vancouver and Victoria became outfitting points for those who took part in the rush. Thousands of adventurers thronged the wharves. Vessels that had been discarded years before as unsuitable for further service were brought back into the trade, and the shipping business enjoyed a boom which it had not known since the sixties. The merchants reaped a harvest of their own. When things had stabilized and machinery and more durable merchandise were required, it was through the merchants of Vancouver that the orders flowed. The economy of British Columbia was given a great boost.

One of the main disadvantages of the coast route to the Yukon was that it had to pass through U.S. territory. Many Canadians, both in Vancouver and in Ottawa, became strong advocates of an all-Canadian route. The most widely publicized of these routes followed the path of the gold-seekers of 1860-61, up the Stikine to Telegraph Creek and then (by land, river and lake) northward to meet the Yukon River at Fort Selkirk. In 1897-98 many proposals came forward to construct a trail and even railroads over this route; the session of the B.C. Legislature of 1897 incorporated no fewer than three such railways. When the excitement died in the Yukon around 1900, railway and trail construction plans were dropped and (as it has years before) the land went back to the fur trade.

In the northwest corner of the province, south of Whitehorse, lies

Atlin Lake. Here in the depths of the winter of 1898, prospectors Fitz Miller and Kenneth McLaren landed on the frozen shores of Atlin Lake and found shallow deposits of gold on Pine Creek. Because their supplies had become exhausted they had to return to their homebase in Juneau, Alaska. But they were back next summer with six other prospectors and staked their claims. Miller subsequently reported to the local newspapers that on his first day's work he took out more than $120 from his sluice-boxes. The news of the discovery quickly spread. During August 1898, prospectors and miners began landing at Atlin Lake — some from Skagway, some from over the pass at Bennett, some from the coastal town of Juneau. By the end of the mining season more than 3,000 people had arrived.

At first Atlin was an isolated tent city, but it was not long before the town had telephone and telegraph systems, with private enterprise adding an electric light-and-power plant.

As with so many other B.C. goldfields, placer mining became worked out and hydraulic mining took its place. This meant the exodus of the individual miner and the coming of the big corporation. There is hardly a long-established mining corporation that has not at some time been interested in hydraulic mining in the Atlin district. For over fifty years from 1898 to 1949 the district lacked road communications with the outside world. Now there is a road to the Alaska Highway at Jakes Corner, and thence to Whitehorse. Gold, the reason for the town's development, is no longer mined there.

Bound for Atlin— the steamer "Gleaner", on Taku Arm in 1900.

British-American Dredging Company's dredge on Gold Run Creek, Atlin, 1903.

General store, Atlin, in depth of winter.

The mining of gold never ceased in the Cariboo. The big hydraulic corporations came in, backed by eastern capitalists with plenty of money to spend in constructing flumes and digging canals to bring enormous pressures of pumped water to wash down the gravel from the hillsides. A result was the Cariboo Hydraulic Mining Company's placer mine at Bullion. At the turn of the century this mine was owned by some of the directors of the Canadian Pacific Railway and was reputed to be the largest placer operation in the world. As a publicity stunt the gold from the big fall clean-up of 1901 was melted at the mine in the form of the barrel of a large naval gun, and shipped to Toronto for display. It weighed 650 lbs., with a value of $178,000.

In 1906 the Guggenheim Exploration Co. of New York, one of the world's great mining organizations, took control and later (according to the Minister of Mines report for 1912) for unknown reasons ordered all work to be abandoned. But it was still working in 1919 under the new ownership of R.T. Ward. It had more than 40 miles of canals and employed 150 men, and was regarded as the largest and best-equipped hydraulic placer operation in North America. In 1932 a Vancouver syndicate stepped in and ran it for the next ten years as a high-volume low-grade placer operation. The amount of water coming out of the hydraulic monitors each day would have supplied the needs of a city the size of Vancouver. There were smaller operations in the Cariboo, like Perkins Gulch Hydraulic (who leased 240 acres in Perkins Gulch at Van Winkle) and the Waverly Hydraulic Mining Co. on Grouse Creek.

On the west coast of Vancouver Island. The mill of the Privateer gold mine, Zeballos, B.C.

Surface plant, with living accomodation in the background. Bralorne gold mine, Bridge River, B.C.

The late twenties saw the emphasis shift to hard-rock mining. In the Cariboo the leader was the Cariboo Gold Quartz, organized in 1927 to work a quartz vein on Cow Mountain west of Barkerville. At Zeballos on the west coast of Vancouver Island, it was the Privateer, first operative in 1938. On Princess Royal Island, halfway between Ocean Falls and Prince Rupert on the inside passage, as far back as 1911, it was the Surf Inlet. In the Bridge River district it was the Pioneer and Bralorne.

66

Gold had been known to exist in the Bridge River country since the days of the pioneer miners of 1858. It was found to be coarser than that of the Fraser and therefore of less value. Most of it was in bedrock and could not be retrieved by the pick, the shovel, or the rocker, so for the next 50 years the Bridge River country held few attractions for the gold miner. What was to become the famous Pioneer Mine was staked in 1897 by Harry Atwood, who had been grubstaked by the proprietor of the Hotel Lillooet. In 1911 it was taken over by a syndicate that spent ten years trying to interest several major companies. Not until Brigadier-General Duff Stewart and Col. Victor Spencer — both prominent Vancouver businessmen — incorporated a new company in 1928 did any meaningful activity start. The Pioneer mine became an outstanding success with yearly production in the millions of dollars. Not very far away was the Bralorne, where Austin Taylor found enough money in the height of the Depression to erect a 100-ton mill. In 1932, Bralorne

Underground— an ore train at Bralorne gold mine, Bridge, River, B.C.

Empire hoist control, Bralorne gold mine, Bridge River, B.C.

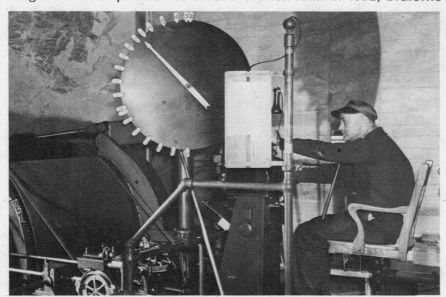

Assayer at work, Bralorne gold mine.

67

sent its first gold brick to the Ottawa mint. In the Depression years, gold mining was the only growth industry in B.C. and much interest was aroused in the Bridge River area. Within the valley in 1933 some 30 companies were testing or developing claims. Minto City, born in 1934, once boasted a population of 800, but by 1942 the mine had petered out. Bridge River became the principal gold-producing center of the province, mining through the Second World War into the sixties; at that stage, rising costs and the fixed price of gold compelled the mines to close in spite of generous government subsidies.

Gold ore wagon from the mines at Wells, B.C.

The only producing gold mine in B.C., as it looked in 1977. A view of surface plant, Northair Mine, seven miles from Brandywine Falls.

The remains of a once-prosperous mine near Lillooet— Pioneer Mine, Bridge River.

The only mine taking out gold in B.C. in 1977. The 3700' level at Northair mine, with ventilating equipment.

Pouring the first gold brick from the Northair mine, June, 1976.

By the end of the sixties all gold mining as an economic activity had ceased in British Columbia. But 1976 saw the first opening of a gold mine in B.C. for many years. The **Northair** mine north of Squamish poured its first gold brick in June, and thereafter maintained a rate of 300 tons per day. A concentrator at the site gives both gold and silver and two of the base metals: lead and zinc.

B.C. GOVERNMENT

A sample of Cariboo nuggets.

69

In the early 1900's road traction engines like this would haul a train of ore cars along gravel roads from mine to railway siding.

4

Progress in Coal 1835~1900

The middle of the nineteenth century was a time when the decision-makers in England were captivated by the marvellous possibilities constantly opened up by new inventions, especially the steam engine. The coal-burning engine became the symbol of the new age. From a means of keeping people warm, coal quickly became a source of mechanical power, displacing the physical toil of animals and men in hauling loads or turning wheels in industry. The burning of coal became essential to the machinery of England's new factory economy. Coal meant power in the physical, economic, and political sense. Countries or individuals who owned or developed coal deposits became the world's industrial leaders.

One of the most profound technological changes that steam brought about lay in the propulsion of ships. No longer did sailors have to depend on the whims of nature — now they had an instrument that enabled them to travel the seas with the certainty that they would arrive in spite of wind and weather within a predictable time. This permitted merchants to trade with countries overseas with an ease and speed never before experienced. It generated a vast expansion of international trade.

The British Admiralty, even in the early days of steam navigation, were sensitive to these changes and looked world-wide for coal deposits to service their new steam navy. Hence the excitement when Dr. William Fraser Tolmie, surgeon-clerk of the Hudson's Bay Company at Fort McLoughlin on Milbanke Sound, learned from an Indian of a black stone that burned near his village. In 1836 Tolmie went to the spot on northern Vancouver Island on the company's steamship *Beaver* and found an outcropping of coal. The find was reported to Chief Factor John McLaughlin at Fort Vancouver and he in turn informed the Governor and Committee in London. In the course of time, Hudson's Bay House in London relayed this information to the Admiralty.

When their Lordships of the Admiralty sent out Captain J.A. Duntze in *H.M.S. Cormorant* in 1846 to the Pacific Northwest, one of his duties was to report on any coal deposits. The captain directed inquiries about coal to the Hudson's Bay officials at Fort Vancouver. Chief Factors Peter Ogden and James Douglas replied on September 7, 1846:

> If the British Government has any intention of making this coal available for use of the steam navy. . .it will be necessary to form an establishment on the spot of sufficient force to protect itself against the natives. . .and also to carry on mining operations.

Other events were fostering the demand for coal in the Northwest. On the settlement of the boundary dispute (which created the Oregon Territory) between Great Britain and the United States, the Navy Department at Washington entered into a mail-carrying contract with William H. Aspinwall of New York for the establishment of a line of mail steamers between Panama and the Oregon coast. Thus came into being the Pacific Mail Steamship Co. One of its more difficult problems was that of obtaining coal for its steamers.

The Mariners' Museum, Newport News, Virginia.

Pacific Mail Steamship Company's Sacramento, 1863.

Aspinwall secured an agreement from the Hudson's Bay Company to open a mine at a deposit known to company officials since 1835 at the northern tip of Vancouver Island if a suitable market could be found. Apparently the market was found; Aspinwall signed a contract for 2000 tons of coal. The Governor and Committee in London then took steps to open up a mine as outlined in a letter dated October 13, 1848, from Sir George Simpson, of the Hudson's Bay Company at Lachine, Quebec, to the board of management at Fort Vancouver, Columbia River:

> "By chartered Vessel which is to sail from London in the course of this month are to be forwarded a headsman and six miners for the purpose of being employed in the coal mine at McNeill's Harbour.

It will be necessary to advise the agent of Mr. Aspinwall at San Francisco of the quantity they may count on receiving at the mine."

This was a milestone in the colony's industrial development: the first export sale of coal from a B.C. mine. John Muir, the mine foreman sent out by the Hudson's Bay Company, employed Indian help to mine the coal but had his difficulties with such inexperienced labor and could not raise enough coal to meet contract demands. A second party of miners arrived in 1852 under Boyd Gilmour. With them came Robert Dunsmuir, the future coal and railway tycoon of Vancouver Island. The **McNeill** (or **Fort Rupert**) mine never became successful — the seams were narrow and the coal of poor steaming quality, as Aspinwall informed his San Francisco agent on May 13, 1850 — so the board of management had to look elsewhere.

The discovery of gold in California and the rapid influx of population opened up very bright marketing prospects for any coal that could be found in Hudson's Bay territory. J.W. McKay, a clerk at Fort Victoria, had told Douglas in 1850 how an Indian had brought a canoe laden with fine quality coal to the fort. It turned out that it came from Protection Island in Nanaimo harbor. McKay had then been instructed to take a prospecting party to look over the ground. They reported findings of coal and in June of 1852 McKay was sent up to make another survey. He found several seams varying from eight to twelve inches in depth. Douglas was able to report to Archibald Barclay, secretary of the company in London, under date of June 23, 1852:

"A bed of surface coal of considerable depth was discovered by Mr. Joseph McKay of the Company's service at Point Gabiola (Gabriola) on the east coast of Vancouver's Island. . . . The principal bed is at Point Gabiola where the seam measures thirty-seven inches in thickness; if so it will be immensely valuable and I will take the earliest opportunity of having it carefully examined and secured for the Company."

He was so impressed by McKay's report that in August of that year he made a personal visit accompanied by John Muir and surveyor J.D. Pemberton. He reported to London on August 18, 1852:

"I rejoice to say that our journey has been productive of very satisfactory results. . . . We discovered three beds of coal. . .from which, with the assistance of the Natives we procured about 50 tons in a single day. . . .This discovery has afforded me more satisfaction than I can express and I trust the Company will derive advantages from it equal to the important influence it must necessarily exercise on the fortunes of this Colony."

Douglas lost no time in occupying and developing the new coalfields. "I have resolved," he wrote, "until I receive the Governor and Committee's instructions on the subject to take possession of the Coal District for the Company and to employ Mr. Muir and two of his sons in opening a shaft."

Joseph McKay was dispatched from Fort Victoria with a party under instructions outlined in a letter written to him by James Douglas on August 24, 1852:

> You will proceed with all possible diligence to Wentubuysen Inlet commonly known as Nanymo Bay and formally take possession of the Coal beds lately discovered there for and on behalf of the Hudson's Bay Co.

> You will give due notice to the Masters of all vessels arriving there and you will forbid all persons to work the coal either directly by means of their own labor or indirectly through Indians or other parties employed for that purpose except under the authority of a license from the Hudson's Bay Company.

The closing of mining at Fort Rupert and the evacuation of the miners to Nanaimo strengthened the work force, but it was not until the end of 1854 and the coming of twenty-two Staffordshire miners and their families on the *Princess Royal* that the mines really began to be worked and the settlement to grow.

Authority to appropriate certain coal lands in and near Nanaimo was sent to Chief Factor Douglas by the Governor and Committee in London in late 1853, with instructions to settle any land claims with the Nanaimo Indians. On December 26, 1854, Douglas advised that he had taken the necessary steps.

The officials of the company, including Douglas, doubted whether the company had the legal power to appropriate land to its own use, now that Vancouver Island was a Crown Colony. Therefore it was resolved by the Governor and Committee in their meeting of May 7, 1855, to purchase 6193 acres in the Nanaimo district from the Colony of Vancouver Island. The purchase price was £1 per acre. The package included most of the land now in downtown Nanaimo, plus Newcastle, Douglas and Cameron Islands in Nanaimo harbor and "the exclusive right to mine for all kinds of coal and coal substances. . .and to keep all such coal and coal substances for the exclusive use and benefit of the Hudson's Bay Company free from any and all royalties or tolls."

For years the company supplied coal to the ships of the Royal Navy and to the San Francisco market. Commander R.C. Mayne, who served in one of the Royal Navy vessels on this coast, wrote in **Four Years in British Columbia**, published in London in 1862:

> There can be no doubt with a liberal outlay of capital under judicious and enterprising management Nanaimo might drive a very flourishing trade at home and with California where coal might be delivered at 12 to 15 dollars per ton. They (the Hudson's Bay Company) mismanaged affairs at Nanaimo. Good and expensive machinery was sent, but sufficient capital to work it was not forthcoming; so that the managers were impeded at the

outset and not enabled to develop the resources of the place. The appliances for delivering coal for instance were so faulty that a ship had to lie there often for three or four weeks before she could take on a load.

To the Hudson's Bay Company it seemed a good time to sell a business in which they had little expertise, one that was in some ways detrimental to their main activity of fur trading. Concerning the coalfield's prospects, an enthusiastic Victoria journalist of the time summed up the situation in this way:

> There is a large demand for anthracite coal to supply Foundries, etc. in San Francisco, Portland, Victoria and other parts, all of which has to be shipped from the Eastern States or from Europe at great expense, the selling price ranging according to quality from $16 to $25 in some markets, in others higher. The trade to Panama and along the Pacific Coast will be considerable and extensive trade will also be opened with China and Japan. The Naval Stations of England, U.S. of America, France and Russia must necessarily consume a large quantity.

Such publicity helped convince a group of moneyed men in the City of London to form a company to purchase the Nanaimo mines. They included Thomas Chandler Haliburton, the noted Nova Scotian author and politician who was a member of the British House of Commons, and John R. Galsworthy, grandfather of the great British novelist of the same name. A representative named Charles Nicol went out to appraise the property. He reported:

> We have got the coal in a bore nearly 5 feet thick. I have now fully proved 1,000,000 tons. With about £5,000 to £8,000 I could start a business doing from 60,000 to 100,000 tons a year. The price is 25sh. to 28sh. alongside the ship. It will give a better idea of the comparative cheapness of this coal if I say that at San Francisco the Nanaimo coal sells for from 12 to 15 dollars while the cheapest good English coal cost, when I was there, 20 dollars.

On the strength of this good news, the Vancouver Coal and Land Co. was incorporated on August 1, 1862, to purchase the Hudson's Bay coal properties at Nanaimo. The package included the townsite of Nanaimo; the mines, machinery, buildings and barges; the islands of Newcastle, Cameron and Douglas; and the right to mine coal in perpetuity exempt from royalties or tolls. From that day began the growth of Nanaimo, as a great coal-mining center, and as the first of B.C.'s planned 'company towns.' The new owners, "being desirous of promoting its growth by independent freeholders," decided to lay Nanaimo out as a townsite and subdivide and sell the lots to private purchasers. The plan, by London architect George Deverill, imaginatively had the streets radiate up the slope from a center close to the shoreline. Many of the streets

The Vancouver Coal Company's locomotive, "Nanaimo". Built in Leeds, England, it was brought out to Nanaimo in 1874, and worked for thirty years in the service of the colliery company.

would remind future citizens of the names of company officials and prominent shareholders. (Wallace Street, for example, came from Charles Wallace, the company's agent in Victoria. Prideaux and Selby Streets both commemorate Prideaux Selby, a company director. Charles Nicol, who became the first resident manager, lent his name to Nicol Street.) The first lots were sold by auction in Victoria in 1864.

Western Canada's first locomotive was brought in to work around the mines. Named *The Pioneer*, it was bought in Lancashire in 1863 — a small standard-gauge saddle tank engine with outside cylinders, 36-inch drivers and a weight of ten tons. The manufacturers sent out two of their own men, Harry Cooper and Thomas E. Peck, to assemble it on arrival and then to run it. Thus they became the first engineer and fireman to run the first locomotive in British North America west of Ontario. The company bought its own steam collier to ship its coals to San Francisco. For many years it ran a highly prosperous concern paying good dividends — 20 per cent in 1868, an exceptionally good year, and an annual average of 10 per cent until 1876.

Several other London-based groups were interested in B.C. coastal coal properties in the sixties. Some three to four miles back of Nanaimo outside the Hudson's Bay limits was the **Harewood** mine, financed by Lt.-Commander the Hon. Horace Douglas Lascelle (commanding one of Her Majesty's ships stationed at Esquimalt) and his associates. It was opened in 1862 under the management of Robert Dunsmuir. This was where Dunsmuir established his pattern — he used similar contacts with naval officers and other techniques to finance and bring into production his great discovery of 1869, the **Wellington** mine.

When coal deposits began to assume commercial importance in the sixties, several companies were organized to look for and develop properties in the Queen Charlottes. One of these was the Queen Charlotte Coal Mining Co. Ltd., incorporated under the laws of the Crown Colony of British Columbia. A party of coal miners was sent out by the company in August 1864 to verify news from the Indians of the existence of coal on Graham Island. They arrived in Skidegate Channel on September 15 and two days afterwards found seams that were four and one-half feet thick. With their supplies exhausted they returned to Victoria with evidence that the coal indeed was there. The company then outfitted and sent out a second expedition in June of 1865, hoping that the mine would be opened up and a wharf and tramway built by April 1866. But these hopes were not realized: food ran out, the natives were hostile, and transportation to and from the islands was (to say the least) precarious. Abandonment of the project can be blamed partly on imperfect understanding of conditions by some of the company officials who had thought "the construction of an easy and inexpensive tramway about one mile in length together with a wharf of about 150 feet projection are all the works (needed) to offer coal in the markets."

Another company, North Pacific Anthracite Coal, organized by Victoria businessmen, sent a civil engineer to Skidegate Bay to survey "a certain tract of land reserved to and for the benefit of the North Pacific Coal Co. by the Government of the Colony of British Columbia at a fee of $400." Transportation was to be provided on a schooner chartered by the company to take goods up to Fort Simpson on the Skeena. Nothing seems to have come of this venture.

In the mid-nineteenth century the thinking of colonial administrators and military and businessmen was spurred by the economic and strategic values of coal. Sir Edward Bulwer-Lytton, Colonial Secretary in Lord Derby's administration, in instructions to Col. R.C. Moody on taking command of the Royal Engineer detachment for duty in British Columbia, directed him to "ascertain the real value of coal for all purposes of steam communication in British Columbia and Vancouver Island."

After Col. Moody had selected the site of New Westminster for the new capital, Governor Douglas sent *H.M.S. Plumper* to survey Burrard Inlet. In the course of this assignment coal was discovered near the entrance on the southern shore of the inlet.

In July 1859, within a month after this discovery, a syndicate of Victoria people applied to the Colonial Government for permission to purchase 5000 acres of anticipated coal-bearing lands situated "on a range of hills between the North Arm of the Fraser River and Burrard's Inlet." Apparently some question arose as to the character of the parties and the request was not granted.

The first concerted attempt to search for coal on Burrard Inlet was made in November 1864 when two prominent businessmen of New Westminster — expressman George Dietz and Sewell P. Moody, the sawmill operator — applied for a grant of 640 acres at English Bay, for the purpose of prospecting and sinking a shaft. Arthur N. Birch, Colonial Secretary at New Westminster replied:

His Excellency (Governor Seymour) is most desirous of facilitating by every means in his power, the successful working of Coal Mines in the neighbourhood of New Westminster. His Excellency is therefore prepared to reserve a tract of land of 600 acres more or less as applied for by you for a period of 6 months from the date of this letter to enable you to thoroughly prospect for Coal.

The promoters set about organizing a company. The results of their efforts, the British Columbia Coal Mining Co. Ltd., came into legal existence on July 22, 1865. Its directors were some of the best known businessmen in the colony: J.A.R. Homer and John Robson of New Westminster, and Sewell Moody, George Dietz, and J.C.

Hughes of Burrard Inlet. The capital ($100,000) was divided into 2000 shares of $50 each. Trouble soon developed with Captain Edward Stamp of Hastings Mill. The impetuous sawmill owner claimed that the company's coal reserve lay within his timber limits. After much argument the coal company surrendered all claims to its reserve on English Bay and took in exchange a plot of land facing Coal Harbor in what is now the West End. A shaft 500 feet deep was sunk but no coal seams of commercial value were found and the work was abandoned. Thus ended, after a loss of $3,000 to the shareholders, the first and last serious attempt to mine coal on Burrard Inlet.

It was a different story on Vancouver Island, where a deposit of good-quality coal was found in the early sixties at Baynes Sound ten miles south-east of Comox. Several attempts at development were made. The Baynes Sound Coal Co. was promoted in Victoria and negotiations entered into with the Chief Commissioner of Lands of the Colonial Government of British Columbia for leases of coal lands. A draft contract leased 5,000 acres for 21 years at an annual rental of $100, but for some reason it was not signed and the project was shelved. In 1875 the company was reactivated and development started. A three-and-a-half-mile tramway was constructed, a wharf and tipple built, and a nine-ton locomotive acquired. A small wooden settlement named Quadra (after the original discoverer of Vancouver Island) went up for the miners. Problems in marketing the coal soon developed and it was not long before the company went bankrupt and the mine closed.

In 1869 came Robert Dunsmuir's great find — the Wellington seam, probably the most profitable and certainly the most productive of all the Nanaimo coal seams. As in the development of the **Harewood** mine, it was a consortium of naval officers (including Lt. Wadham Diggle) at Esquimalt who put up the money to bring it into production in 1871. The **Wellington** mine of Dunsmuir Diggle & Co. became one of the best known on the Pacific coast. Like the Vancouver Coal company's mines, it built up a large market with San Francisco.

The **Wellington** colliery was situated three miles west of Departure Bay. At first a tramway using wooden fir rails was built to bring the coal down to the wharf at Departure Bay. It was gravity operated; the loaded cars in descending pulled the empties back. In 1874 two steam traction engines from the Admiralty in London were shipped out to Nanaimo and changed to locomotives by adding flanged wheels. They replaced the gravity system on the tramway, relaid with iron rails. The machines, even by the standards of those days, were cumbersome and difficult to operate. They had a flywheel six feet in diameter, with one cylinder on top of the boiler and chain gears to the two driving wheels. Four years later they were retired and replaced by two small 0-6-0 saddletank engines — the *Duke* and *Duchess* — built by Baldwin's of Philadelphia. The *Duke* had been on display at the Centennial Exhibition at Philadelphia where Robert Dunsmuir purchased it. Dunsmuir Diggle & Co. placed an order for a second one of *Duke's* design and both arrived in Nanaimo in 1878. These engines worked for the **Wellington** colliery for many years; the *Duchess* until 1899 when she was bought by Captain John Irving and sent north to Atlin, and the *Duke* until it was scrapped in 1909.

First train from departure Bay to Wellington in 1880.

There were now two big coal companies dominating the picture in the Nanaimo area: the Vancouver Coal Co. and Dunsmuir Diggle & Co. In the last 30 years of the nineteenth century the Vancouver Coal Co. opened and closed several mines. The company stayed up-to-date; it was the first on the Pacific Coast to use a diamond drill, and always seemed to be able to open a new mine when an old one had to be closed. Gradually the shafts sunk by the Hudson's Bay Company on the seafront in what is now downtown Nanaimo were closed. A new one — the **Douglas** pit, a little further inland — was then opened along with the **Fitzwilliam** mine on Newcastle Island. The most famous of all Nanaimo mines — **No. 1** on the Esplanade, the mainstay of the town for 50 years — opened in 1881 when the **Fitzwilliam** closed. **Chase River** opened in 1877 and closed along with the **Douglas** pit in 1885.

Over the years a network of colliery railroads grew up around Nanaimo. It has been noted how the Vancouver Coal Co. brought out its first locomotive in 1863. This was followed by a second named the *Euclataw* after a small Indian band living nearby. It operated for 36 years in the company service, mainly in taking ballast from the ships. Next to appear was the *Nanaimo*, one of the classics of B.C. railway history. It was built in Leeds and came out from England in 1874. In 1884 came the first 20-tonner from the Boyne Engine Works of Manning Wardle & Co., the great engine builders of Leeds. Vancouver Coals's first U.S. engine came from Baldwin's in 1891. It was an 0-6-0 type with 48-inch drivers and weighed 35 tons. Three more Baldwins followed, and established world records for loading coal into waiting steamers. One day in the late nineties, the steamer *Titania* loaded 5,800 tons from the Vancouver Coal wharf at Nanaimo for San Francisco in the time of ten-and-a-half hours — a world record.

The other great colliery company, Dunsmuir Diggle & Co., for many years only operated the **Wellington** mine. It soon turned to U.S. makers for its motive power. After the *Duke* and *Duchess* came the *Robert Dunsmuir* from Baldwin's in 1883, the *Departure Bay* in 1887, and the *Victoria* in 1889. Three other Baldwins were purchased when the Chandler interests of San Francisco closed down their mine at East Wellington. They were the *Premier*, built in 1878, and the *East Wellington* and the *San Francisco* in 1883.

These colliery railways provided many skilled jobs that would not otherwise have been available in such an undeveloped country. The maintenance and repair of miles of track and the operation and servicing of over a dozen locomotives and some hundreds of coal cars kept a force of skilled workmen constantly employed.

Dunsmuir Diggle & Co. soon started to export to San Francisco in competition with the Vancouver Coal Co. It was the only market, other than ship bunkering and a small demand in Victoria, that the coals of Vancouver Island enjoyed. English partners contracted for and had built in a shipyard near Newcastle-on-Tyne an iron steam collier of 3,000 tons. This vessel, named the *Wellington*, carried hundreds of thousands of tons of coal from Departure Bay to San Francisco. In the early seventies the trade was most profitable, netting in some years from $6 to $8 per ton. When the price in San Francisco fell to $8, Dunsmuir tried to reduce the contract price he paid his miners to 81 cents per ton. This was not a living wage and the white miners — over 150 of them — refused to work. Dunsmuir then prepared to import strike-breakers from San Francisco and asked for protection from the government. Through the efforts of Lieutenant-Governor A.N. Richards and the Attorney-General, The Hon. A.C. Elliott, *H.M.S. Rocket* was dispatched from Esquimalt to Departure Bay. The sheriff, on Dunsmuir's orders, tried to evict the miners and their families who rented company houses at **Wellington**. Violence flared up and he and his men had to retreat. Then both the government and the miners' committee tried to persuade Sir Matthew Begbie to arbitrate the issue but he refused. In a characteristic policy statement, Dunsmuir bluntly told the Attorney-General in a letter from Departure Bay of March 9, 1877, that he "would not allow anyone to arbitrate on our business as I can manage that myself and in fact there is nothing to arbitrate on except the breaking of the law by the miners."

Finally, under Dunsmuir's threat that "if the law cannot be carried out I shall have to shut down the works for 12 months," the Attorney-General ordered in the militia. Lt.-Col. C.F. Houghton, deputy adjutant-general of Military District No. 11, called out the total effective militia force in B.C. — the Victoria and New Westminster Rifles and the Seymour Battery. They arrived at Departure Bay on May 2, 1877, and sped to **Wellington**, where the sheriff completed his evictions without further incident. Many miners were arrested and sent under escort to Victoria to appear in court.

Seven received prison sentences and the remainder a caution. The strike collapsed and the miners returned to work under Dunsmuir's terms. This was the first of a series of bitter disputes between Dunsmuir and his miners which culminated in the widespread disorders of 1913-14. Thus the Dunsmuirs, both father and son, began to acquire their reputation as ruthless, forceful, and uncompromising employers.

After the settlement of the strike, to entrench themselves further in the San Francisco market, Dunsmuir Diggle & Co. opened their own sales office in that city. Here Dunsmuir met the U.S. railway magnates Collis Huntington, Charles Crocker and Leland Stanford, the shrewdest railway promoters in the business. It was no doubt with their help that he was able to buy out his English partners to transform the firm into R. Dunsmuir & Sons. These three California tycoons enabled Dunsmuir to obtain the charter and build the Esquimalt & Nanaimo Railway, which in later years played such a large part in developing the coal industry on Vancouver Island. They also made is possible for the railway to obtain a substantial land grant that aroused much opposition among the Canadian people. In the Canadian House of Commons, M.P. John Charlton sprang to the attack in the session of 1891:

> There was a little line of railway . . . along the sea coast from Victoria to Nanaimo a distance of 70 miles the construction of which was scarcely necessary; to promote the construction of that railway nearly all the coal lands of the Island of Vancouver were granted to a syndicate the greater proportion of the capital being held in San Francisco by the Southern Pacific Railway magnates. . . . The lobby influences here, the backing here, were too strong, the grant was made, the coal lands have gone.

There is no doubt that the Esquimalt & Nanaimo Railway fattened the Dunsmuirs' interests. When the **Extension** mine was opened in the Wellington seam in 1895, the railway was used to take the coal to shipping points. The **Cumberland** field, opened by James Dunsmuir in 1889, benefited when the railway reached Union Bay and Comox. Expertise in railway construction and management could always be drawn by the coal company from the staff of the Esquimalt & Nanaimo Railway at a nominal cost. No systematic program of exploration for coal lands ever seems to have been developed by the railway company. In fact, prospectors and mining engineers interested in exploration were discouraged. When the land grant was purchased along with the railway by Canadian Pacific in 1905, much of it lay unexplored and unsurveyed.

Coal operations around Nanaimo had to contend with many unusual conditions resulting from the field's geological character. The irregular distribution of good seams made for high costs in mining and handling. In many cases it was impossible to use machinery for cutting. The instability of the seams often prevented the use of electrical equipment and explosives. The Royal Commission on Explosions in Coal Mines reported in 1903: "In mines where mechanical haulage is employed, especially where electric motors are used, the motors and trains of loaded cars almost fill the area of the roadway and when going at full speed obstruct the passage of free air." The cost of extra work in hauling and washing ran at 75 cents per ton of coal. Shale and sandstone were intermingled with the coal and had to be brought to the surface and separated. Miners were often docked 25 per cent of the tonnage for waste, a continual source of grievance.

The increased output in the later years of the nineteenth century was made possible only by the expenditure of large sums of money for underground and surface plants, washing, handling and loading facilities. Even so, the average annual production always trailed behind that of mines in Washington State or the East Kootenays.

In ocean transportation both companies owned some colliers outright and chartered many others. They were the first on the Pacific Coast to use the new type of whaleback boats originally designed for the Great Lakes grain trade. The whaleback steamer *Wetmore* came to the West Coast in 1890 and loaded coal at Nanaimo for San Francisco. A year later, engaged in the same trade, it ran ashore near Coos Bay in Washington State and became a total loss. Steamers of this type never became common in the Nanaimo-San Francisco coal trade.

Typical Whaleback Boats

A report in the Victoria *Colonist* of March 31, 1891, reads:

> The first mining company in Canada to call electricity to its aid in the practical development of the working of its property is the New Vancouver Coal Co. Mr. Roblins, the manager, is reported to be looking into the installation of underground electrical haulage in his mine.

82

On June 23, the *B.C. Commercial Journal* followed up:

> J.S. Anderson, district agent for the Edison General Electric Co. has just closed a contract with S.M. Roblins, the superintendent of the New Vancouver Coal Co. to place in the company's mine in Nanaimo an electric tramway and light and power equipment.

Thus is recorded the earliest use of electricity and electric traction in any coal mine on the West Coast.

The Nanaimo mines in the early days were notorious for bad ventilation and inflammable gases. In 1884, 23 miners were killed in a gas explosion in **No. 1** pit of the Vancouver Coal mine on the Esplanade. Three years later an explosion and a fire at the same mine took 147 lives. At Dunsmuir's **Wellington** colliery on January 28, 1888, an explosion crippled the hoisting cage and left 168 men underground. After three hours' work, rescue crews managed to get the cage moving again, but only 91 men came up. Thirty-one whites and 46 Chinese were missing. On February 15, 1901, at the **Union** colliery in Comox, an unexplained explosion killed 64; not one miner working underground came out alive. In the same year 16 were killed at **Extension** by a fire. For the ten years from 1894 to 1903, there were 843 accidents, 437 of them fatal, reported in B.C. mines in a work force of approximately 4000. In this period one out of every five miners was involved in some kind of mine accident. In relation to the tonnage produced, the accident rate was higher than in Great Britain or the United States.

The philosophies of management held by the two great coal companies in the Nanaimo area were widely different. The directors of the Vancouver Coal Company were knowledgeable London professionals. They were practical men, followers in the liberal tradition of John Morley and W.E. Gladstone. When they laid out the townsite of Nanaimo it was not simply a company town they wished to create (although they had before them the world-famous example of Saltaire, outside of Bradford, where Sir Titus Salt had just completed a model town for his workpeople) but a town for "independent freeholders." Company policy was to hire experienced miners in England and assist them to come out and settle in Nanaimo. When Vancouver Coal acquired the **Harewood** mine and estate the company set aside five-acre lots to be leased to employees with an option to purchase, hoping to provide more support for the miners in bad times when work was erratic. After the great disaster at **No. 1** pit in 1887, about 175 widows and orphans received free housing and fuel from the company for as long as necessary. In contrast with the Dunsmuirs, Vancouver Coal recognized and bargained with a miners' union as far back as the early 1890s. It solved a bitter grievance by appointing union instead of company men as coal weighers (check-weighmen), ensuring that output was honestly weighed and recorded by a fellow-worker.

Through the writings of John Galsworthy the personalities and problems of the Vancouver Coal Co. were portrayed in fictional form. In Galsworthy's great classic of middle-class Victorian life, **The Forsyte Saga,** the character of 'Old Jolyon' Forsyte was based on the character and experiences of his father, who was company chairman. To investigate the affairs of the company at first hand, Galsworthy spent much time around Nanaimo talking to miners and company officials and acquiring a stock of experiences that he incorporated into many of his writings. In the short story 'Silence' and the play *Strife*, personalities and incidents relating to Vancouver Coal Co. can be identified.

The company built up a reputation for being progressive and fair-minded, with a sense of social responsibility as practised within the framework of mid-Victorian society. This was in sharp contrast to the attitude displayed by the Dunsmuirs. If the attitudes of the directors of the Vancouver Coal Co. can be designated as liberal, those of Dunsmuir and his partners were distinctly conservative. The rights of property — Dunsmuir company property — took first place.

Robert Dunsmuir's youth had been spent in the coalfields of Ayrshire, at a time when the Scottish coalmine owners exercised almost feudal rights over their miners. He matured in the authoritarian atmosphere of the Hudson's Bay Co. Coming up the hard way under the harsh British system, he ran his business with a view to the greatest productivity for the least outlay. He exhibited no real interest in his workmen and their conditions. Unlike the Vancouver Coal Co., who went out of their way to hire experienced miners, Dunsmuir would hire anyone who would work for him. The inexperienced Chinese, as they would work for very little pay, were highly favored, and sometimes kept the mines open when white miners refused to work. Like many other leading British and U.S. industrialists of the time, he was against all unions and would fire any man who held a union card. Grievances remained unsolved for years — like the controversial weighing of each miner's daily output, a practice that the miners claimed short-weighted them, and frequent reductions in the contract price paid for coal. The hostility between the parties was shown in the bitter strike of 1877 and then again in 1889-90 when troops were quartered in Wellington (at James Dunsmuir's request) for five months at company expense.

B.C.'s coal-mining industry was not an unqualified success. The yearly value of coal production passed that of placer gold in 1883, making it the leader and greatest revenue producer in the province's mining industry. It contributed a major part of the total mineral wealth of the province for the next thirty years. In 1889 the Dunsmuirs went into Cumberland and Union Bay and erected coke ovens which supplied coke for a few years to the smelters at Crofton and Ladysmith. But the operators had unfavorable conditions to contend with: coal of inferior quality, much mixed with shale and sandstone, with a limited domestic demand and a long haul (1500 miles) to face stiff competition in the nearest international market. The Nanaimo coalfields lay far from the centers of technological advance. To bring in up-to-date machinery, with the skilled help necessary to service and operate it, was a major problem both technically and financially. It is surprising that the colliery owners were able to install the type of equipment that they did, and B.C. has good reason to be grateful to them.

Coke ovens at Comox. Dunsmuir's Union Colliery.

The railway that gave Robert Dunsmuir access to the best coal lands on Vancouver Island. A passenger train crossing the Niagara Canyon trestle on the Esquimalt & Nanaimo Railroad in May, 1900.

5

Change & Turmoil on Vancouver Island

Most British Columbians felt that the dawn of the twentieth century revealed a prospect of increasing well-being, of widening opportunities to individuals ready to develop their province. An ever-higher standard of living seemed built into the system. Time-honored values and institutions were evolving slowly, at a pace that gave time for adjustment. Trade and travel were relatively free from restrictions over wide areas of the world. In business, the rise of new industries created a demand for basic materials that could be satisfied only with difficulty. The mining of coal, to fuel the factories and run the expanding transportation systems, increased many times over. For British Columbia it was the start of unprecedented wealth.

It was then that James Dunsmuir started to develop his **Extension** mine a few miles southwest of Nanaimo. Coal, an extension of the Wellington seam, was reportedly found by a Mr. Hobson in 1894. Details of the find were never made public, but it is said that Hobson found a tree uprooted by a storm with the coal bed nestled underneath. James Dunsmuir sent in his surveyors, who found a seam nine feet thick at its tip and running to eleven feet as it went deeper. As it lay on Esquimalt & Nanaimo Railway land, Dunsmuir had no difficulty in claiming title. One of his companies, the Union Colliery Co., did some extensive prospecting in 1896 and shortly afterwards coal began to be shipped out.

Dunsmuir intended to ship the coal out through his existing facilities at Departure Bay, by building a spur from **Extension** to his railroad from the **Wellington** mine. Grading had actually started before the discovery was made that the line would cut across land owned by the New Vancouver Coal Co., which refused permission. In those days there was no Railway Expropriation Act and

Dunsmuir would have had to wait for a special bill at the next sitting of the House in Victoria. While he certainly had the political clout to achieve passage, this might have damaged still further his relations with the citizens of Nanaimo. He turned elsewhere for deep-water facilities where he could build coal bunkers and a loading wharf. The location finally picked was Oyster Bay where Ladysmith now stands.

Large coal bunkers (holding 8000 tons) and a loading wharf went up at the new site in 1898. From the mine a spur line met the Esquimalt & Nanaimo Railway two miles north of Oyster Bay.

Coal passed along this route for more than a year before any plans were drawn up for a townsite at Ladysmith. (Meanwhile about 200 miners — mostly single men — had built shacks and houses around the pithead at **Extension**.) The decision to build near the bunkers was made at the start of the Boer War in the winter of 1899. George Pinder, a veteran civil engineer who had been with the Esquimalt & Nanaimo Railway since the days of its construction, was given the job of laying out the new townsite. As yet it had no name. The story is told that James Dunsmuir and George Pinder were looking over the site in March, 1900 when a telegram was handed to them announcing the relief of Ladysmith

Birds-eye view of present-day Ladysmith.

from the Boers. Dunsmuir turned to Pinder and said,"That will be the name of this place, but be sure you name the streets appropriately." The original townsite plan named each street after a famous British general: Methuen, White, Baden-Powell, Roberts, Gatacre, Buller, Kitchener. It provided for only twelve blocks — not enough to accommodate the 4000 people who would flock to Ladysmith within a couple of years. Forty more blocks were opened up in August, 1901.

The sudden decision to open up this Esquimalt & Nanaimo Railway land for intensive settlement was influenced by Dunsmuir's closure of the **Wellington** mine. Some 800 miners from **Wellington** were moved into Ladysmith to work at the **Extension** mine, bringing their homes with them on flatcars. From an output of 40,000 tons in 1899 to 267,000 tons in 1900 and 405,000 in 1901, the **Extension** mine developed into one of the big producers on Vancouver Island.

In 1901 the miners still living in **Extension** were told in no uncertain terms that they would have to vacate and live in Ladysmith. Some had been living there for five years and were unwilling or unable to leave. The order, direct from James Dunsmuir, was blunt and to the point: either move to Ladysmith or get out. A few reluctant miners were fired and others were given deficient places where rock and dirt predominated over coal. The rest quickly found ways to live in Ladysmith and commute by the miners' train. This caused bitter resentment and was one of the factors contributing to the strike of 1903.

More problems were looming. Faulted seams with large amounts of rock and dirt kept wages below those of other local miners. Favoritism by the pit bosses was another grievance. Miners who curried favor or were related to the bosses were given locations where the coal was thicker; Samuel Mottishaw, a Nanaimo miner and leader in union activities, said of the **Extension** mine that he had never seen a greater inequality in wages.

Things got to such a point that the miners became desperate; in spite of the well-known attitude of James Dunsmuir towards unions, they organized a local (No. 151) of the Western Federation of Miners. The company swiftly posted a notice (on March 10, 1903) that all miners had to take their tools out of the mine within three weeks, and in the meantime the executives of the local were dismissed. The miners, 800 of them, voted to strike and authorized a committee to go to Victoria and see James Dunsmuir. Dunsmuir left a record of what happened through his testimony to the Hunter Commission on Industrial Disputes:

> They sent in their card and said they wanted to see me. I sent out to them to ask if they represented the Western Federation of Miners and they said they did and I sent back word that I could not see them. That was the end of that committee.

The miners stayed out another two months, but when funds ran out and there was no other work to go to, they voted to return at a reduction of five per cent in wages. The company refused to re-employ the union officials so the miners had to abandon their affiliation with the Western Federation of Miners. It was another incident in the bitter struggle that peaked in the troubles of 1912-14.

The Union Colliery Co., created by Robert Dunsmuir to develop the mines in the Comox valley, had an 1888 charter of a somewhat restrictive nature. It was legally confined to the coal business, and Dunsmuir's business had so broadened in the intervening years that it was no longer a suitable instrument for carrying out his objectives. In the winter of 1902 a new company was created. The Wellington Colliery Co. Ltd., capitalized at $2,000,000 ($1,700,000 fully paid up), was owned almost entirely by James Dunsmuir and was granted unusual powers. It could engage in practically the whole spectrum of business activities including those of a trust company. Of the 20,000 shares issued, James Dunsmuir owned 19,900 in his own name. The other directors held only 25 shares each. The new company took over the operating mines in the Comox district and the **Extension** and **Alexander** mines and their auxiliary services.

James Dunsmuir tried in several ways to bring other businesses to Ladysmith, which was never intended to become a company town. A transfer wharf was built for the Esquimalt & Nanaimo Railway to make Ladysmith the terminal for barging all freight cars to and from the mainland. The Tyee Copper Co. received land to build their smelter for treatment of Mount Sicker ores. (There was a touch of self-interest here, as the smelter would use Wellington Colliery coal in the form of coke — roasted in the company ovens at Union Bay and transported by Dunsmuir's ships.) The company provided practically nothing in community services. It was only after the incorporation of Ladysmith, for example, that the council was able at last to bring in electric light.

As company policy dictated that all miners live in Ladysmith, the station usually presented a busy picture. The railway was the life blood of the town and the mine, but despite the density of the mine traffic (12,000 tons of coal per week) there were few accidents. The most serious was that on September 16, 1900, at a bridge two miles north of Ladysmith, when two coal trains met head on and killed four people.

The year 1903 was a disturbed one on the B.C. labor front. There was discontent among the miners working in the Wellington Collieries at **Cumberland** and **Extension.** The United Brotherhood of Railway Employees had struck the C.P.R. at Vancouver. The coal used on the C.P.R. ships came from **Cumberland** and railway workers were anxious to cut off the supply. They were eventually able to do this with the help of the Western Federation of Miners, a

U.S.-based international union. Through the locals of the Western Federation in **Cumberland** and **Extension,** the mines were closed either (as Dunsmuir claimed) in a lock-out or (as the Federation claimed) in a strike. As a result, the C.P.R. had to bring 10,000 tons from Japan to fuel its trans-Pacific liners at Vancouver.

In Nanaimo the New Vancouver Coal Co. had long held a reputation as a progressive company and a good employer. Most of its miners were of English or Welsh stock and English visitors who stopped over in Nanaimo had nothing but praise for the company and the community. In 1902 the editor of the *Leeds Mercury* offered this first-hand report to his readers:

> I have never seen coal miners so comfortably placed as those in Nanaimo. Their lodgings are not in miners row. Every miner has his own house and some of their abodes...were more elegant and commodious edifices than those of many well-to-do first class families in England. About 100 have acquired five-acre homesteads. The majority prefer to reside within the city limits where they have lots 66 ft. wide and 150 ft. long but all own their own homes.

How the Western Fuel Company housed their miners. Company houses at Brechin Colliery, near Nanaimo.

Life in Nanaimo at the turn of the century was rich and full. Sport was much emphasized, with soccer the great game. Teams of the caliber of the English first division played against Cumberland, Ladysmith and Victoria. Cricket, played on a company-donated field, was very popular. There was an amazing variety of cultural societies. The arts, music and drama were enriched almost weekly by the visits of professional groups from the mainland or the United States. The churches were busy, and many a week-night saw services by well-known evangelists.

Late in 1902 the miners employed by the New Vancouver Coal Co. became concerned about rumors of change in ownership. On December 18, 1902, the *Nanaimo Free Press* displayed banner headlines across its front page: "Nanaimo Collieries Sold — Western Coal Co. of San Francisco Buys Out Local Collieries." No more important news for Nanaimo could have been announced. The Western Coal Co. purchased outright all real and personal property of the New Vancouver Coal Co. at a purchase price around $650,000 — far from the $11,000,000 which Mackenzie & Mann paid Dunsmuir for his coal properties eight years later.

The new owners of the coal mines of Nanaimo were striving to obtain a monopolistic position in the coal trade of the San Francisco Bay area. They sought to become a local trust in coal, just as the United States Steel was nationally in steel. The coal mines of Nanaimo had become entangled with the trusts and monopolies so prevalent in the United States at that time.

The miners up in Nanaimo had reservations about the new owners. Would they follow the paths of Carnegie or Rockefeller or Dunsmuir in their labor-management policies? In December of 1902 they organized local 177 of the Western Federation of Miners, the first Nanaimo miners' affiliation with an international union. Western Fuel promptly recognized the new union and signed an agreement to guarantee $3 per shift for miners working in spots where the coal seam was deficient or too much mixed with dirt and rock to enable a miner to earn a fair day's wage. This was the first time in the history of Vancouver Island coal mining that any type of guaranteed wage had been given.

Old Canadian Bank of Commerce Building, Nanaimo.

Bank of California, San Francisco.

In **Cumberland** and **Extension**, the miners were driven back by hunger and lack of funds. After the great strike of 1903 some eight or nine years went by when unionism in the coalfields was very much on the decline. Competition in the San Francisco market from the Washington State mines became fiercer; in some of these years Puget Sound exported more in tonnage than all the Vancouver Island mines. California oil was now being brought north and infiltrating the B.C. coastal market at the expense of the

Vancouver Island mines. As the *Nanaimo Free Press* put it in an issue of December 22, 1902:

It was not the decrease of the quantity of coal exported but the uncertainty as to the final and permanent effects of the oil competition upon the coal trade which has caused money to be locked up and put a stop to almost all but the most necessary expenditure and prevented investment in new enterprises.

Even the Minister of Mines in Victoria, in his annual report of 1902, first took note of the oil competition:

When it is considered that a large proportion of the output of the coast mines is used in California and that petroleum fuel has been introduced into that State to so great an extent it is remarkable that the falling off (of coal shipments) has been so slight.

The mine owners realized that sales patterns were changing and the future of the industry might be in jeopardy. For example, sales of Vancouver Island coal to B.C.'s coastal cities increased from 25 per cent of total production in 1902 to 71 per cent in 1912. Exports to the United States (mainly San Francisco) over the same period fell from 70 per cent of production to 21 per cent. The booming factories of the lower mainland, and the large business blocks which had sprung up in such a surprising manner in Vancouver, as well as domestic needs for many thousands of new homes, consumed the coal that used to go to California. For the first time, coal was shipped in substantial amounts to off-shore markets other than the United States. Mexico in 1912 took more Vancouver Island coal than the total exported in 1876. Ship bunkering, formerly one of the mainstays of the industry, was now in rapid decline as more vessels turned to oil.

These shifts and uncertainties were highlighted when James Dunsmuir put his coal properties on the market and developed the biggest financial deal that had ever taken place in B.C. It involved two great U.S. railway systems, a Canadian corporation, Wall Street capitalists, and financiers and fund-raisers in London. It all started on January 8, 1910, when Dunsmuir instructed R.T. Elliot (a Victoria lawyer) to find a purchaser for his coal properties. A Portland representative of the Great Northern and the Northern Pacific railways acquired an option on the properties and found his way to financial backers on Wall Street: J.P. Morgan & Co.

News of these activities soon became known to other interested parties in Victoria. For some time both William Mackenzie and Donald Mann had been in close consultation with Sir Richard McBride and the provincial cabinet about building a third trans-provincial railway through B.C. to link up with Alberta. They became interested in the Dunsmuir properties for both economic and political reasons and set up a company (the Canadian Collieries (Dunsmuir) Ltd.) to take them over.

Even though the interest charges on the newly issued bonds almost amounted to the profit that Dunsmuir had been earning on his coal properties in good years, Canadian Collieries at once embarked upon expansion and modernization. Designs were prepared for an electric power plant to be built to service the mines in the Comox coalfield as well as the towns of Cumberland and Union Bay. (This plant, the Pultney hydro-electric project, came on stream in 1913.) The English investors enjoyed two good years when dividends on bonds and preference shares were paid out of profits earned; then profits plunged in 1913 and it was not until 1928 that bond-holders gained any further benefits. The shareholders, both preference and common, lost all their equity.

B.C. MINISTRY OF MINES

Portal of the Tsable River mine of Canadian Collieries (Dunsmuir) Ltd., near Comox.

B.C. GOVERNMENT

Western Fuel Company's coal tipple, Nanaimo harbor.

While Dunsmuir was disposing of his coal properties the C.P.R. was not idle. In April of 1910 it was appraising the property of the Western Fuel Co. with a view to purchase. It also showed interest in the smaller mines around Nanaimo — like the Pacific Coast

Coal Mines Ltd., which ran the **Morden** mine at South Wellington with a mineral railway 7½ miles in length to Boat Harbour. This company, established in 1907, had mineral rights over 7000 acres and produced some 600 to 700 tons of coal per day from its property. Investigations appeared to come to nothing, possibly because the owners were asking too high a price. The Western Fuel Co. also figured in a story carried by the *San Francisco Call* in July 1910, when it was reported that a British syndicate was negotiating for the property at a profit to the Californians of more than $2 million — an attractive offer, considering that the property only cost them slightly over half a million dollars. It was one more indication of values now being placed on real estate and industrial property in this province.

The New Vancouver Coal Co. was now an American corporation and there was always the fear that at some stage its management would wield the big stick. This fear never really became a reality until the troubles of 1913. They treated their employees in the same humane way that the old company had shown. When the crunch came in the summer of 1913 the United Mine Workers had great difficulty in getting workers there to strike in support of all the other Vancouver Island mines.

Ironically, the growing awareness of the Vancouver Island miners of the hazards under which they worked, combined with the efforts of the lawmakers and the Department of Mines at Victoria to relieve those hazards, was the spark that initiated the longest and most bitter strike in the annals of labor in B.C.

After many years of agitation, the miners in 1911 had obtained the legislated right to elect or appoint a committee that could (at their own expense) inspect the tunnels of the mine in which they worked for dangerous pockets of gas. Such a committee had been elected at the **Extension** mine; it found gas pockets in the mine and these findings were confirmed by a government inspector sent in by the Department of Mines.

When Oscar Mottishaw, a committee member, had worked out all the coal from the spot assigned to him by the pit boss he was refused another place to continue working. He left **Extension** and found a job as a mule driver in the **Cumberland** mine. After a couple of days the contractor received instructions from the mine superintendent to fire him. It turned out that Mottishaw was a member of the United Mine Workers of America, which complicated matters — the union tried to take the matter up with the mine management, who refused to discuss it. Mottishaw then approached management himself, but was told by the superintendent that the company "reserved the right to hire and discharge unquestioned." All the old bitternesses, the unresolved grievances came to the surface: the favoritism of the bosses, the assignments to deficient places, the shovelling of coal for unreasonable distances, the lack of facilities for proper weighing, the inability in many cases to make a living wage. The miners voted to take a holiday until Mottishaw was reinstated; the company acted in its usual way and posted what amounted to lock-out notices.

The **Cumberland** mines closed down on September 15, 1912, beginning the most expensive strike in B.C.'s history. Violence, injuries, arrests and imprisonments characterized the strike from the outset. Two days later the **Extension** miners were out. The company brought in special police and strike-breakers and, with the help of Chinese and Japanese workers who had stayed on the job, gradually got back to a reasonable level of production.

For the first seven months, only the miners who worked for Canadian Collieries were on strike. They had the backing of a powerful international union, the United Mine Workers of America. It claimed a membership of 400,000 and was well able to provide strike pay and trained organizers to support a comparatively minor walkout involving 1500 to 2000 miners. After a few months a strike-breaking force at Canadian Collieries, with the protection of the special company police, brought the **Cumberland** mines back to almost normal production. **Extension** was unable to get back to pre-strike production levels. The company was moving along very nicely, however, satisfying the domestic market with some importation of coals from Washington State. The union was in a bind: it could not carry on the strike indefinitely and the company was in no mood to negotiate. It therefore decided upon a calculated risk in an effort to close the industry down completely. In Nanaimo they had very little support, as the Western Fuel Co. enjoyed good relations with its local union.

This was the situation on April 30, 1913, when Frank Farrington, United Mine Workers official and strike co-ordinator for Vancouver Island, wrote the president of District 28 U.M.W.A.:

> I hereby instruct you to call a strike of all men employed in and around all the mines at Nanaimo, South Wellington and Jingle Pot, the strike to begin May 1st and to continue until a joint working agreement between the United Mine Workers of District 28 and the mine owners of Vancouver Island has been secured.

On the following day notices went up at all Nanaimo mines declaring a strike. The Nanaimo miners came out but their wisdom was questioned by many. A meeting of the Western Fuel employees mainly made up (it is claimed) of above-ground workers and clerical staff voted by a majority of eighty-five to stay on the job. This did not deter the underground workers and the mines closed down. About 3800 men were now off the job in all the mines in the Nanaimo and Comox fields and tensions mounted.

Within a few days the Jingle Pot mine in Nanaimo, run by the German company promoter Alvo von Alvensleben, signed a contract with the United Mine Workers. Throughout all the remaining troubles it ran a model operation with union support and none of the interruptions that affected the other mines. The big companies still imported strike-breakers and reinforcements of special police. Crowds up to 300 strong began to parade the streets of Nanaimo and Ladysmith. Strike-breakers going to or from work were often accompanied by crowds of 50 to 100 jeering miners.

Loading coal into cars.

Where the troops first landed at the time of the labor troubles on Vancouver Island, August, 1913. Brechin Colliery near Nanaimo.

In Nanaimo things were swiftly coming to a head. On the afternoon of Monday, August 11, some 600 to 700 people assembled at the pithead of No. 1 mine on the Esplanade to meet strike-breakers coming off the afternoon shift and stoned the cars taking them away. On Tuesday the crowd had grown to 1000 and more stones and lumps of coal were thrown, injuring several. Wednesday was a day of crisis, when crowds at the wharf turned back the specials coming over from Vancouver on the Princess Patricia and sent them back on the same boat. Then they gathered 700 or 800 strong outside the office of the *Herald*, whose editor had been on the side of the owners. Into the midst of the crowd galloped a boy on a horse crying that six strikers had been killed at **Extension.** This sent them off in a body to **Extension,** where combined forces of strikers from Ladysmith and Nanaimo drove the strike-breakers down into the mine or out into the bush. Burning and looting began at dusk, with 23 white miners' houses either burnt or looted and **Extension** Chinatown completely wrecked. Wives and children of the strike-breakers had to flee into the bush and remained there for two or three days with scanty clothing and no food until they were rescued by the militia.

In Ladysmith, in the words of Judge Frederic Howay, one of the presiding judges at the subsequent trials of the strikers, "Bombs were thrown, property was destroyed, houses were damaged, peaceable citizens were driven from their homes and made to flee. A consistent course of terrorism was indulged in." Crowds of strikers roamed through the town on what they called "peace missions," advising the people to take an excursion. (According to Judge Howay, this meant "that a band of lawless people went around the city ordering peaceable citizens out.")

Rioters were in complete control. Crowds went to strike-breakers' homes and gave them until high noon on Saturday to get out. Window-smashing brigades were organized; a bomb landed in the house of Alex McKinnon, a one-time union member who had gone back to work, maiming him for life. The arrogance of union members was such that Duncan McKenzie, a leader in the disturbance, gave the police a list of the people that the union wanted driven out of Ladysmith. The president of the local, J.J. Taylor, told one concerned citizen, "We are the law and you got to go." By the end of the week all semblance of civil control in the Nanaimo-Ladysmith area had been removed.

At Victoria, Attorney-General William Bowser called for military aid. It arrived on August 14, in the form of two Victoria militia units: the 88th Victoria Fusiliers under Lt.-Col. A.J. Hall and the 5th B.C. Regiment of Garrison Artillery under Lt.-Col. Arthur Currie, who commanded the Canadian Corps in France four years later. These units, 1000 strong, left Victoria by the night C.P.R. boat at 2 a.m. and landed without incident at Western Fuel's Brechin mine. Such was the fear in Victoria that the movement of the troops

Damage caused by the strikers. The mine entrance at Extension, August, 1913.

The commanding officer in the Nanaimo area, Colonel John A. Hall of the 88th Regiment, and some of his officers, at Nanaimo in August, 1913.

A troop train on the Esquimalt & Nanaimo Railroad at Duncan, enroute to Nanaimo in August, 1913.

An Army Service Corps unit encamped at Nanaimo.

They came well-armed: A Maxim machine gun, somewhere near Nanaimo.

B.C. PROVINCIAL ARCHIVES

Part of the Vancouver contingent. A group of 72nd Seaforth Highlanders in camp at Nanaimo.

might be impeded that all telegraph and telephone communication with the upper island was cut off.

The strikers were taken by surprise as the troops moved into Nanaimo. Companies of soldiers were dispatched to **Extension** and the people in hiding were rescued. Troops 450 strong were sent from Vancouver to Cumberland and to Union Bay, where efforts had been made to burn the wharf. Hall took over the telephone and telegraph offices in Nanaimo and used a company of Seaforth Highlanders to send messages over the wires in Gaelic, a code that baffled the union leaders. For a short time the military tried to censor all messages from the Nanaimo area, giving a foretaste of what was to happen in the coming world war.

To shatter union power, the military considered it necessary to arrest all the unionists who could be considered active in the disturbances. The next union meeting in Nanaimo found the troops surrounding it. Car lights were trained on the doors; as union members emerged they were taken into custody at bayonet point. Many others were picked up in the next week or two at Extension and Ladysmith and even as far south as Victoria. More than 200 were arrested, most of them being kept in jail without bail. For some days a state of war existed in the coalfields.

The militia broke the back of the strike. The companies were able to run their mines without hindrance, using imported strike-breakers. The continued presence of the militia enabled them to ignore their striking miners and concentrate on manpower and production. Many of the strikers received stiff prison sentences because, in the words of Judge Howay, "This thing in which you engaged was not an ordinary riot." A widespread view suggested that it was not solely an economic struggle between employers and workers, but also an attempt by powerful U.S. union leaders to change the pattern of society in the coalfields and bring socialism into Western Canadian society.

A few militia units remained on duty for over a year — until August 1914, when more pressing military problems presented themselves. Through the efforts of Sir Richard McBride, Minister of Mines, a settlement on company terms was reached that month, two years after the initial walkout. Miners were rehired if places could be found for them. In the words of Henry S. Fleming, president of Canadian Collieries (Dunsmuir) Ltd., in his annual report of 1914:

> Since that date nearly all your Company's employees who were on strike have applied for reinstatement and their applications have been duly filed in the several offices. Owing however to the depressed business conditions which have been accentuated by the war in Europe our previous working force has been sufficient to produce all that the market has required and thus far only a small number of strikers have been re-employed.

During and after the troubles many left to take up farming or logging or emigrated to the mines of Washington State. Those who stayed suffered extreme privations, especially the wives and families of those in prison. Requests for clemency to the provincial government by unionists in other trades in British Columbia fell on deaf ears. Public appeals for support for the victims of the strike were made, but the strike and its consequences were quickly forgotten in the war effort.

World War I gave a few more years of grace to the slumping coal-mining industry of Vancouver Island. The surge of industrial activity on the Pacific coast in 1916 and 1917 created a short-lived abnormal demand. Postwar oil from California proved a stronger and stronger competitor. The ship-bunkering trade continued its decline. Whereas in prewar days 80 per cent of the vessels engaged in ocean shipping used coal, in 1924 the number had fallen to 20 per cent. Although there was plenty of coal in the Nanaimo coalfield, it has often been overlooked that the coal seams were erratic and hard to find; even harder was the task of keeping track of market conditions, which mitigated against high-cost mining. In the face of all this, mine-owners were surprisingly persistent and successful in keeping the mines open and finding markets.

One of the most hopeful signs of a postwar regeneration of the industry came with the interest in the Nanaimo coalfields shown by the Granby Consolidated Mining & Smelting Co. Immense quantities of coke were needed to fuel the furnaces of the huge copper smelter that the company had just completed at Anyox, and the company wanted complete control over its coke supply. In cooperation with the Esquimalt & Nanaimo Railway, company engineers uncovered what appeared to be a good seam of commercial coal nine miles south of Nanaimo at Cassidy. But then

GRANBY MINING COMPANY

The entrance to Granby's model mine at Cassidy, Vancouver Island.

101

a dispute arose over the title to this land, which was included in the area of the railway land grant but also had been granted by the Crown to a settler before 1883 and duly bought by Granby. The railway company and Canadian Collieries (who held coal-mining rights over all of the Esquimalt & Nanaimo land grant) contested ownership in the courts. At stake were coal-mining rights over the whole Esquimalt & Nanaimo land grant, purchased by Canadian Collieries from James Dunsmuir in 1910. The case involved years of argument in the courts. In the meantime the mining company had taken steps to open up the Cassidy mine and to build a model settlement to house its workers, a relatively new concept that it had recently used at Anyox.

Nanaimo harbor. Western Fuel Company's coal loading wharf, with French steamer at left, 1920.

Cassidy's well-designed townsite featured houses with three to ten rooms, of designs similar to those in the better-class suburbs of Vancouver or Seattle. On completion in 1918, they sold for $2,500 to $7,000. For single men, a large rooming-house offered 80 rooms, all opening to the verandah or balcony and equipped with steam heat, electric light, and hot and cold running water. Everything possible was done to attract and keep a stable work force. The responsibility that the company felt and its efforts to brighten the lives of its employees was recognized in the Minister of Mines annual report for 1919: "A striking feature of the company's plans in laying down ideal conditions under which the men shall work is the programme of entertainment and physical and mental relaxation provided."

The plant housed the most up-to-date machinery. Power was generated on the spot through an Allis-Chalmers generator supplied with steam raised in two water-tube boilers fired by mechanical stokers. (The power house chimney, 125 feet high, was built in 12 days by an outside contractor.) Electric storage-battery locomotives supplied traction in the mine. Coal was loaded into wooden mine cars built locally in the company shops. It was

Coke ovens of the Granby Consolidated Mining & Smelting Company at Anyox, supplied by coal from the company's mine at Cassidy on Vancouver Island. 1927.

shipped over Esquimalt & Nanaimo tracks to Ladysmith and barged up to Anyox for coke. A little high-quality domestic heating coal was sold to the trade in Vancouver or Victoria. By 1920 the company had its own loading wharf ready at Ladysmith.

The underlying idea, naturally enough, was to bring out the maximum amount of coal at the least cost. Coal faces with abnormal dirt content were left intact. Despite this, there were so many faults in the coal seam that at times only 20 per cent of the tonnage was in coal. Outbursts of gas within the mine occurred with increasing frequency. There were 60 of these blow-outs in 1922; the largest displaced 1500 tons of coal and continued to give off methane gas for the next 72 hours. Employment peaked in 1922 at 498, stayed around 250 for a year or two, and then averaged off at 225.

At the height of the Depression in September 1932, after a 50 per cent drop in production over eight years, the decision was made to close the mine permanently. The parent company, Granby Consolidated, was building up at Anyox a stockpile of copper which it could not sell. Today the townsite has vanished. The buildings that could be taken away were removed under the hammer of an auctioneer in 1936. Those so solidly built that they could not be moved became covered over by the underbrush. Part of the townsite was excavated for a gravel pit by the B.C. Dept. of

103

Highways. No trace is left of the shady streets with their comfortable houses and well-kept lawns. Thus ended an early attempt by a big foreign corporation to provide acceptable standards of living to its workers in an isolated B.C. area.

After World War I the Canadian Collieries, so heavily capitalized that it could not meet the interest on its indebtedness, fell into the hands of the bondholders. Shareholders lost everything. Mackenzie & Mann withdrew and the bondholders in London took over in a re-organization that wrote down the assets by $9 million. The committee in London held tight control over capital expenditures; no improvements came into the business, equipment became obsolete, markets declined, and not until the bondholders had been paid off in 1947 did the company's prospects brighten. In that year a group of Vancouver businessmen took over. They gradually eased the company out of the coal business and went into gas and oil exploration (in which they made a substantial profit) and then into forestry. They sold out to Weldwood of Canada, a subsidiary of the giant U.S. Plywood Corporation, in 1964.

The banner years for the Island's coal industry were probably 1918 to 1923, at least in numbers employed. Production did not climb much above the figure of 1912, but employment in the industry

Looking north to Nanaimo, about the time the last coal mine closed.

B.C. GOVERNMENT

rose to 5100, the highest level it was to reach. From 1923 to the start of the Depression, production dropped as much as 100,000 tons a year or more, and employment dropped with it — from over 5000 to 3500 in 1929. Fuel oil began to take more and more of the energy market. Vancouver Island coals not only had to compete with Peruvian and Californian oils, but also with coal brought in from Alberta. Canadian Collieries was now the dominant figure. It bought out Western Fuel in 1928 and controlled all the major collieries. Out of the 2000 people employed in the mines in 1937 Canadian Collieries employed 1860. It was still the biggest employer in Nanaimo and Cumberland and paid out $2,000,000 a year in wages.

In the Depression many of the famous mines closed permanently: **Extentsion** in 1931, **No 4 Comox** in January and **South Wellington** in May of 1935, **No. 1 Esplanade** in 1938. The remainder were working only two-thirds of the time. With a staff of 1625 the Vancouver Island mines in 1934 produced 575,000 tons, the lowest figure in 60 years. The Second World War brought temporary relief while industries that had been using oil turned back to coal, but there was a serious shortage of skilled labor and the mines could never get back into the stride of prewar production. After the war years, the industry never regained its dominance. Everybody was using oil. By the end of 1953 all the major mines in the Nanaimo area had closed and Canadian Collieries moved its staff and head office to Cumberland. Individual miners would still work some of the smaller mines and bring out a few tons daily, but the days of the big coal-mining and big companies on Vancouver Island had gone.

Inspecting coal seams on Johnson Creek in the Peace River coal field, in the early years of this century.

6

Province ~ Wide Black Diamonds

Coal is found in many places in B.C. Some 53 large deposits span the province from the Laird River drainage basin on the Yukon border to Crow's Nest in the southeast straddling the Alberta border. All the major fields are so far removed from the larger ports that overseas shipment is difficult. The four most important areas are the East Kootenay basin, the Peace River in the vicinity of the western foothills of the Rocky Mountains, the Telkwa-Bulkley Valley field in and around Smithers, and the Groundhog basin in the Stikine River area 150 miles north of Hazelton.

Minor fields include Bowron River, 30 miles east of Prince George (estimated to contain more than 25 million tons of coal), and Hat Creek, 15 miles from the British Columbia Railway near Ashcroft.

In southeastern B.C. the Kootenay coalfield stretches more than 100 miles north from the U.S. border, and is thought to have almost unlimited resources of coal. At Sparwood-Fernie where the Kaiser Resources Ltd. are now working, 230 square miles are underlain by coal; the length of the field is about 34 miles and its maximum width 12 miles. The original promoters of the field, the Crow's Nest Pass Coal Co., had estimated its reserve on two limited areas of 15 square miles at over a billion tons. The Elk River basin north of Fernie, where the Fording Coal Co. is now working, extends some 50 miles with a maximum width of 10 miles. (The rich coal-bearing seams of the Upper Fording River have been known for 90 years or more.) One authority puts the approximate reserve in the Elk River basin at 3½ billion tons probable and a further 2½ billion tons possible. At many locations the coal deposits are close enough to the surface to encourage strip mining. This field is one of the few in B.C. with high-quality coking coals.

The Peace River coal beds are more than 160 miles in length and 10 miles in width. The field lies around the town of Chetwynd, 60 miles west of Dawson Creek and 80 miles by road from Fort St. John. Mines in this district have been worked in a small way since 1940. Today it is an area of high potential, the Quintette properties of Denison Mines Ltd. being of particular interest.

The Telkwa-Bulkley Valley deposits range in area from seven square miles close to the C.N.R.'s line at Telkwa to 20 square miles of coal at Coal Creek at the headwaters of the Zymoetz River. These claims were developed between 1912 and 1914 by Copper River Coal Claims Ltd., but the project closed through lack of capital.

An area that for many years aroused great interest, especially from some of the greatest South Wales coal owners, is the Groundhog

Coal Creek Colliery, Kootenay district, 1926.

field some 150 miles north of Hazelton. The area covers 170 square miles with an estimated coal reserve of 900 million tons.

Two official estimates of coal reserves in B.C. have been made, the first by D.B. Dowling of the Geological Survey of Canada in 1913 and the second by B.R. MacKay of the same agency for the Coal Commission of 1946. The Commission came up with a figure of 11 billion tons of which 5½ billion tons was recoverable at that date.

The first mention of coal in the interior of British Columbia seems to have been made by Father Jean de Smet, a Roman Catholic missionary to the Kootenay Indians. In a letter written about 1845, he notes having seen lumps of coal in the waters of the Elk River. It was another thirty years before anything was done about it — by Michael Phillipps, a long-time employee of the Hudson's Bay Company who was discharged when the company sold its posts in the western United States. He turned to prospecting and in 1874 came into the Crows Nest country with a party that included Jim Morrissey, a miner. They went up the Elk River and took some coal out of a creek which they named Morrissey Creek. The next creek they named Coal Creek because, in Phillipps' words, "We could find nothing but coal and coal everywhere." Coal was of no value to them — it was gold that they were looking for.

William Fernie, one of those adventurous spirits who opened up the West, had worked both for the government and private

The headquarters for the first great coal development in eastern British Columbia, the Kootenay town of Fernie.

Abandoned coke ovens of the Crow's Nest Pass Coal Company at Morrisey, B.C.

B.C. GOVERNMENT

contractors in the Kootenays since 1864. He went prospecting every summer, accompanied by Col. James Baker and armed with information supplied by Michael Phillipps, and had registered many coal claims in the Elk River district. Col. Baker, an M.L.A. who ran a farm and store where Cranbrook now stands, formed a syndicate to develop their Kootenay coal properties.

The coal wealth of the Kootenays was now becoming known, partly through the publication in 1885 of Dr. George Dawson's report of his preliminary survey of the Rocky Mountain country south of the projected line of the C.P.R. Dawson, who had received coal samples from the Phillipps' find, placed great stress on the coal seams on the Bow River area to be traversed by C.P.R. line. He also mentioned coal seams noted in the Crow's Nest Pass. In a report to the Commissioner of the Royal North West Mounted Police of 1886, Superintendent Sam Steele of the Fort Steele detachment wrote of "the value of the coal lands in the pass, its suitability as a railway route and the lightness of the work in comparison with that of the Kicking Horse Pass."

The man who drew the attention of Toronto capitalists to the coal resources of the Kootenays: Dr. George Mercer Dawson, 1849-1901, Director of the Geological Survey of Canada.

The attention of Ontario entrepreneurs turned westward again. Louis Riel's uprising had put the West on the front page of every newspaper in Central Canada creating new interest in western development. The Galt interests, intimately connected with the Conservative party and Sir John A. Macdonald were active in the Canadian Northwest and especially in the coal mines around Lethbridge. A new breed of moneyed men was emerging in Toronto in the shadows of such new Ontarian banks as the Canadian Bank of Commerce and the Dominion Bank. George A. Cox was a native-born Ontarian who had won his place financially by his management of the Midland Railway of Canada. He was interested in many of the great financial institutions of Toronto, helping to make Bay Street the financial center of Canada, and pioneering with industrial firms in the new technologies. In 1886 he and several of his associates organized the Crow's Nest Pass Coal Co. to prospect and develop the coal lands. They were in close touch with Baker and Fernie.

For several years the two local experts had organized parties at Fort Steele for surveys of the coal lands of the East Kootenays. In 1886, with the Hon. F.W. Aylmer, they incorporated in Victoria the Crow's Nest & Kootenay Lake Railway Co. to build a "Railway from some point in Michel Creek . . . hence by the Elk River to the Upper Kootenay River, thence by way of Cranbrook and the Moyie Pass, and the Goat River to the Lower Kootenay River."

A great coal mining region, and the location of one of Crow's Nest Pass Coal Company's collieries— Michel, B.C.

It was capitalized at $4,000,000 but only $10,000 had to be paid in to set it up in business. A separate bill of the same date granted the company "a right-of-way through the lands of the Crown 99 feet wide." Surprisingly, the land grant did not include mineral rights. It may be assumed that the proprietors had already found and marked out the best coal lands. To acquire these they formed a syndicate and set up the Crow's Nest Coal & Mineral Co. Ltd. Its charter empowered it not only to deal in coal lands, but also to serve as a colliery. The company's position in Victoria was strengthened by bringing in Joseph Despard Pemberton, a veteran land surveyor who had surveyed the original Nanaimo coal mines for the Hudson's Bay Company.

The crossing of British Columbia by the C.P.R. and the anticipated wealth of minerals in the Kootenays had stimulated the interest of many people in opening up the country by new railways.

Provincial legislators from 1886 to 1890 found their time taken up largely with private railway bills sponsored by promoters after land grants. In 1890 a railway aid bill was passed granting land subsidies to several proposed railways, one of which was the Crow's Nest & Kootenay Lake. The usual 20,000 acres for every mile of railway was included in its grant; unfortunately, some of the best coal land had already been given away. The land south of the Elk River had been handed over to the federal government and transferred to the C.P.R. A private company, the Kootenay Valley Co., had also acquired holdings. To make up the deficiency in the Crow's Nest & Kootenay's subsidy, its land grant included:

> A belt of land five miles in width along the east side of the Elk River extending between a point five miles below Morrissey Creek and a point twenty-eight miles above Michel Creek and from a belt two and one half miles in width on each side of Coal Creek extending to the summit and from a belt three miles in width on each side of Michel Creek and on each side of the east and west branches of the said creek to the summit.

Thus Col. Baker, William Fernie and their associates picked up some of the richest coal lands in the East Kootenays at an initial cost of $10,000.

The omnibus land-grant bill made no mention of coal-mining rights to the land seceded, but stated that "nothing in this Act shall prejudice the rights of free miners to search for, get and win the precious metals — subject to the mineral and land laws of the Province."

The richest coal lands in the Province were of no value without transportation to take the coal to the markets. Thus the efforts of the syndicate for the next few years were devoted to finding someone who could build the railway for them. They went back to Victoria year after year for extension of time and amendments to their charter. A significant change came in 1893 when all their coal and railway interests in the East Kootenays were consolidated under a new railway, the British Columbia and Southern. The turning point was in 1896 when the Liberals came into power in Ottawa. George A. Cox, Robert Jaffray and their associates in Toronto were great Liberals in federal politics and now could exert much influence. Under the name of the Crow's Nest Pass Coal Co., the Toronto group took over the British Columbia and Southern Railway charter.

Van Horne and Shaughnessy of the C.P.R. had for some time been anxious to break into the Kootenays and take the business that

Dr. Alfred Cecil Selwyn of the Geological Survey of Canada, active in investigations of the Elk River coal field in 1891.

GEOLOGICAL SURVEY OF CANADA

now was going to Spokane. But they needed a railway charter and there was no better one on the market than Cox's B.C. Southern. The lawmakers at Victoria gave their statutory permission for the B.C. Southern to extend its line to Fort MacLeod and Lethbridge and lease it to the C.P.R. A Special Act designated the railway "of general advantage to Canada" under a perpetual lease. It was a beneficial arrangement for all parties: the Crow's Nest Coal Co. got the coal lands it wanted at a nominal cost, the C.P.R. got its railway subsidized into the Kootenays, and B.C. was assured of benefits to taxpayers from mineral development in the southeast. The land grant to the B.C. Southern came to 3,750,000 acres, almost double the amount given to Dunsmuir for the Esquimalt & Nanaimo. Of this total the company kept or disposed of 1,200,000 acres and in 1912 sold back to the province 2,540,000 acres at the price of 40 cents per acre.

Following in the footsteps of Dr. George Dawson, in 1891 Dr. Alfred Selwyn of the Geological Survey of Canada made another survey of the Crow's Nest coalfields.

> There is (he reported) in the Crow's Nest Pass between the eastern summit 4330 feet above tide and the valley of the Elk River in British Columbia an area of not less than 144 square miles that is destined to be one of the most valuable and most productive coal fields in Canada.

B.C. GOVERNMENT

B.C. MINISTRY OF MINES

The country in which the Canadian Pacific Railroad developed a coal mine in pre-World War I days—Hosmer, B.C. Mount Hosmer in background.

Newly-erected steel tipple, Hosmer coal mine, Hosmer, B.C. 1908.

Apart from the C.P.R. grant around Hosmer and the B.C. government's reserve of 50,000 acres, all the coal lands up the Elk River for about 60 miles and through Crow's Nest Pass to the Alberta border was owned by the Crow's Nest Pass Coal Co. When the railway became assured in 1896-97 by the agreement reached by the C.P.R. and the federal government, the company started to open up its mines. Samples of coal from Coal Creek were found excellent for coking. Development began in earnest in 1897 at Coal

Creek under the supervision of William Blakemore, recently appointed general manager. Blakemore had been mining engineer for the Dominion Coal Co. in Cape Breton and had pioneered cutting machinery in their mines. He had persuaded several experienced Nova Scotian miners accustomed to the mining life to come west with him and they formed Coal Creek's working core.

The equipment was the finest in the West. Mine haulage underground was done by 10-ton electric locomotives and run by an overhead trolley system.

This extensive project 70 miles from the nearest settlement (Fort Steele) presented housing problems. Uneven ground made it impossible to build a town or coke ovens at the mine, so a town was planned for the projected junction of the colliery railway with the C.P.R. track on the eastern bank of the Elk River; it was named after William Fernie, now land commissioner for the company. By 1902 every lot on the new site had been sold. Fernie was not a company town, although the company claimed ownership of the land. From July 1898 to January 1902, the company sold 211 lots for an average of $277 per lot.

Conditions at this time were very primitive. Water had been piped in by the company from Coal Creek primarily for their own use, but was supplied at a price to the citizens. Conditions were so unsanitary that fears had been often expressed that an epidemic of typhoid fever would arise. It was not until 1901 that the town enjoyed electric light, furnished by a company so loaded with Crow's Nest Pass Coal directors and officials that it was just a lengthened shadow of the coal company. In spite of the efforts of the company to house its miners closer to their places of work, Fernie became the commercial center of the coal-mining district.

At the mine site at Coal Creek (six miles east of Fernie) and Morrissey (seven miles south), considerable settlements grew up. At Michel, 25 miles to the northeast, somewhat later a number of townsites arose near the mine with their own stores, hotels and saloons.

The company ran a big operation: its own railway connected its three mines with the C.P.R., its coke ovens operated at Fernie, Morrissey and Michel. In 1899 it employed 400 miners; by 1902 the number had grown to a couple of thousand. Payrolls ran from $130,000 to $150,000 per month. Company towns were built at Morrissey Mines and Michel, and liquor licenses (which were under company control) seemed to be granted with a free hand. In 1902 Morrissey Mines had ten — with a population of 100.

Life in the coal towns was rough and tough. In the early days the towns were little better than camps. Housing in general was poor, built without basements or plumbing and on wooden blocks for easy removal. In the areas that housed newer arrivals from many countries, slum conditions prevailed. The liquor traffic was so bad that the merchants continually protested over the miners' inability to pay their bills. The company seemed unwilling to control this abuse; although no hotel could be opened in a company town without company permission, this was seldom withheld. The region had been well known for its lawlessness ever since construction days. Bank managers travelled armed, occasionally with police escorts. Their staff could often be found at target practice with revolvers.

A custom which caused quite a little concern was the miner's habit of putting the blasting powder in the kitchen oven in damp weather to keep it dry. Cases have been known when he or his wife cooked dinner and forgot to take out the dynamite — with disastrous results.

The greatest danger was fire. Settlements and towns of the early days, built entirely of wood, were prime targets. Volunteer fire companies were early institutions, with firemen's hose-laying races and ladder-climbing events as popular sports. Fernie experienced two disastrous fires. On April 29, 1904, its six-block business section was wiped out. But the greatest blow was the complete destruction of the town in three hours in the early days of August 1908. A forest fire struck the town and some 3000 people barely escaped with their lives after a wild unscheduled train ride to a sandbank on the river bed five miles from town. Railway cars and tracks, coal and coke stocks and company equipment were all lost in the greatest forest-fire disaster ever suffered by a B.C. town. It became a national news event and money poured in to help the sufferers from many points throughout the nation and the United States.

Crow's Nest coal and coke found a ready market in the smelters of the Kootenay and the Boundary country. After the **Morrissey** mine was opened up to the United States market in 1902 via Great Northern Railway, the difficulties of the company were not in selling but in production. The company produced its coke in 1900 at $3.50 per ton and sold it at $4.25 in a market where the smelters had been paying between $15 and $16. Imports of coke into B.C. virtually ceased.

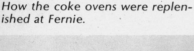

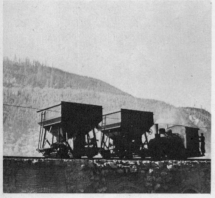

How the coke ovens were replenished at Fernie.

B.C. MINISTRY OF MINES

Coal mining operations, as practiced by the Crow's Nest Pass Coal Company in the Kootenays.   B.C. MINISTRY OF MINES

Right: Tipple at Corbin, 1909.

Left: Michel Colliery, Crow's Nest Pass Coal Company, 1909.

B.C. MINISTRY OF MINES

Stripping by steam shovel, Corbin Colliery, Corbin, B.C. 1927.

As the new century began much coal prospecting was done in the East Kootenay field. The C.P.R. had its crews out surveying its properties and eventually opened up a mine on its property at Hosmer, six miles north of Fernie in 1908; by 1909 it was prospecting in the Fording River area. A railway line had been surveyed into the valley of the Upper Fording River from Michel. Private companies such as Northern Coal & Coke and Imperial Coal also had parties in the field.

At the same time D.C. Corbin, now well into his sixties, opened up a mine on McGillivray Creek. The development was really a by-product of the new railway that Corbin was then building: the Spokane International. The C.P.R. was deeply interested in this railway and lent its influence in raising money for the mine development. A spur 14 miles long (the Eastern British Columbia) was built from the mine to the C.P.R. tracks. Entirely oriented to the U.S. market, the underground mine serviced steam plants and industrial users in the Inland Empire and also the Spokane International Railway. After World War I, as markets declined, the technique was changed to open-pit mining with the use of steam shovels. Like many another mine, it was closed permanently by the Depression. Its miners rounded off its career hand-picking the coal from the surface for their own domestic heating.

115

How the survey and development crews in the Groundhog coal field were supplied— Catalines pack train leaving Hazelton, pre-World War I.

One of the spin-offs of the Klondike gold rush was the survey work of the federal Department of Railways and Canals in Northern B.C. on railway routes through Canada into the Yukon. Expeditions went out from Edmonton in 1898, 1899 and 1900. They did some geological work and sent back rock specimens to the Geological Survey of Canada. V.H. Dupont, a member of one of these parties, explored the Peace River Canyon in 1898 and no doubt picked up some coal-bearing rock to send back to Ottawa. In 1899 he made the first recorded discovery of coal in the **Groundhog** fields north of Hazelton. In 1903 an ambitious program of coal prospecting in the Peace River country was mounted by Col. Roderick R. McLennan, a former railway contractor and a private Ontario banker. Furnished with letters of credit on the Hudson's Bay Company's northern posts the party followed the Peace River to its canyon, where they set up camp and prospected for over a month. They enjoyed many adventures including a hair-raising trip down an unprecedented length of the canyon in a home-made raft.

The trip was not entirely unsuccessful. Coal had been found in considerable quantities and Col. McLennan filed his claims with the government and kept them in good standing until it was definitely known that the Grand Trunk Pacific Railway would go through the Yellowhead Pass. The fact that the Peace River country had been set aside more or less as a government reserve since Confederation put a damper on prospecting or development well into the twentieth century.

Swimming pack train animals over the Stikine River at Telegraph Creek.

In the **Groundhog** field 100 miles north of Hazelton, James McEvoy and his assistant W.W. Leach, working on behalf of the Western Development Co.—a Toronto syndicate underwritten, it was reported, by the Crow's Nest Pass Coal Co.—surveyed and staked 16 square miles of coal lands in the years 1903-04. Getting in and out of the field was the problem. The district was hundreds of miles from any settlement and occupied the height of land around the headwaters of three major rivers: the Skeena, Stikine and Nass. Pack-trains took a month to make the round trip to Hazleton. The trail was not open until late spring and closed in early fall, so only three or four trips could be made per year. Reports suggested, though, that it might turn out to be one of the most important coal-bearing areas in the province.

In 1912 William Fleet Robertson, provincial mineralogist, was instructed to visit and report on the field. His difficulties in reaching the locality pointed out the problems inherent in development. On August 16, 1912, he wrote: "After seven hours travelling in which only fourteen miles were covered, camp was made." On arrival he found some 600 miles of coal-bearing land had already been staked. A company, the B.C. Anthracite Coal Syndicate, had a party in the field and had already surveyed 50 square miles. Another company with claims was owned by Alvo von Alvensleben, the German promoter and financier working from an office on Hastings Street in Vancouver.

B.C. MINISTRY OF MINES

An early wooden bridge in the Stikine country.

After World War I, with a depressed industry in the south, interest in the northern fields vanished, though Dr. A.F. Buckham and B.A. Latour spent the summers of 1948 and 1949 in the **Groundhog** area on behalf of the Geological Survey of Canada. Spurred by Japanese demands, such fields as the **Peace** and **Groundhog** are now receiving the attention so long deferred. Interest was aroused in 1976 by the building of the Dease extension of the British Columbia Railway, graded to within 20 miles of the coal area that year. No coal licenses were yet granted by the provincial government but several major companies were expressing interest.

Much northern activity has centered in the foothills district of the **Peace**. The Quintette properties of **Denison** Mines appear to be the most likely area, with production slated for 1981 involving one of the best reserves of coking coal within the province. Mitsui Mining Co., a subsidiary of the great Japanese trading organization of Mitsui, has supplied some of the exploration capital for what could develop into a thriving surface mine with an annual production of three to four million tons.

The **Saxon** property in the same region, also under coal lease to **Denison**, is being vigorously prospected; up to $1,000,000 of exploration money was allocated to it in 1976. The European consortium Exploration und Bergbau has a large interest in this venture.

Utah Mines Ltd., a great U.S. copper company already working a large copper mine on northern Vancouver Island, since 1971 has been in the Carbon Creek district and East Mt. Gething—the country that was first prospected by the Robert McLennan party in 1903. Sizable reserves of coal have been found there, but they are not expected to come into production soon.

Some 70 miles south of Chetwynd lies the area which until June of 1976 was under option to the Coalition Mining Co. (Brameda Resources). Test mining was done for a number of years but now the cption has been handed back to the Teck Corporation, the coal lessee of the property. British Petroleum has now purchased the property and is planning to produce ½ million tons per year within the next 2 or 3 years.

The greatest deposit of thermal coal in the province lies in the Hat Creek area between Lillooet and Ashcroft. Exploration dates back to 1957 under the auspices of the privately owned B.C. Electric Railway Co. The B.C. Hydro and Power Authority, now owners of the property, began the present exploration program in July 1974 and reserves and resources are now estimated at over 2 billion tons. The seams have proven 1000 feet in thickness and could long support a liquefaction plant to turn coal into oil on the South African model or be used simply as thermal coal.

In the Crow's Nest area as markets declined and the Depression eroded trade, the mines closed one by one. In spite of federal subsidies, reductions in pay and company economies, the Crow's

After the blast— coal ready to be hauled away at a Peace River coal mine.

Power drilling in a Peace River coal mine, northern British Columbia.

Examining a sample of coal from the Peace River country.

Nest Pass Coal Co. passed through difficult years. It was not until the 1960s and the extraordinary comeback of the Japanese economy that interest in Crow's Nest coal revived. With the advent of the bulk ocean cargo carrier, the unit train and better handling equipment, it became possible to export B.C. coal to Japan at competitive prices. For a number of years small shipments had been sent through the port of Vancouver to the Japanese steelmakers from both the B.C. and the Alberta side of Crow's Nest. In 1964 Kaiser Steel, a multi-national corporation with interests in steel, aluminum and industrial minerals, bought most of the land holdings of the Crow's Nest Pass Coal Co. (now Crow's Nest Industries). These included coal rights on about 108,000 acres in the Fernie-Sparwood area. The Mitibushi group of trading, steel and mining companies

119

supplied a firm market — 4,750,000 tons of coal each year until 1985. Kaiser put up most of the development capital, aided by a consortium of U.S. and Canadian banks, and the Canadian public was invited to participate through a public offering of shares. Under the 1973 refinancing program the Japanese purchasers of Kaiser Resources coal acquired a 27-per-cent equity interest in the firm.

On the territory that had witnessed the first coal development in the Kootenays, Kaiser opened a large strip mine and underground operation using a new technology — pioneered by both the Japanese and Russians — of hydraulic mining of coal. A coal terminal was built at Roberts Bank near the Fraser River estuary some 20 miles from Vancouver. The C.P.R. strengthened its track and put on unit trains carrying from 10,000 to 12,000 tons. For some years the operation was in doubt both financially and technologically, but the problems have been resolved. This operation alone brings some 4,750,000 tons annually to Roberts Bank for export. The Canadian Pacific interests, with Cominco as development overseers and now operating managers, Canadian Pacific Investments as financial agent and fund-raiser, and Canadian Pacific Rail as the transportation arm, have brought into production a 2,000,000-ton-per-year export operation on coal lands held under license in the Upper Fording River. They are also selling to the Japanese steelmakers.

Interest now is very keen in the East Kootenay fields. North of the Upper Fording the European exploration consortium which is also interested in the Saxon property in Northern B.C. is exploring some 17,000 acres in partnership with Scurry Rainbow Oil Ltd. For the first time an Ontario steel company, Stelco of Hamilton, holds a considerable interest (25 per cent).

Down in the Flathead country near the U.S. border where D.C. Corbin of Spokane pioneered a coal mine, Rio Tinto Mines of London (England) through their Canadian subsidiaries is diamond drilling and bulk sampling a property at Sage Creek which will give an estimated three to four million tons per year.

Finally, Crow's Nest Industries — the first in the field — is evaluating an open-pit operation with its Japanese partner Mitsui Mining at Line Creek.

This renewed activity in British Columbia coal is attributable not only to the energy crisis and the uncertainties of world oil supplies at prices that Western economies can stand, but also to the restrictive attitude now taken in the field of coal development by the Alberta government. Apart from Kaiser Resources and a few small freeholders in the Princeton-Nicola area and on Vancouver Island, all potential coal reserves are on Crown land. Those that are now being developed and worked are under coal licenses — **Fording Coal**, Crow's Nest Industries at **Line Creek**, **Denison** Mines and Rio

Stripping the overburden at Kaiser Resources' open pit mine at Sparwood. Note the size of the dump truck.

Tinto's **Sage Creek**. Hence the coal policies of the B.C. government are extremely important. The government is anxious for industrial development and eager to attract local or foreign investment into coal-mine development. The future looks bright.

One of the reasons why eastern British Columbia coal can be sold to Japan. A 10,000 Canadian Pacific Rail coal train, on the way from Sparwood to Roberts Bank, near Vancouver.

CANADIAN PACIFIC RAIL

Coal loading equipment at Roberts Bank.

KAISER RESOURCES

B.C. GOVERNMENT

Roberts Bank, the new superport near Vancouver. Used jointly by Kaiser Resources and Fording Coal for the export of Kootenay coal.

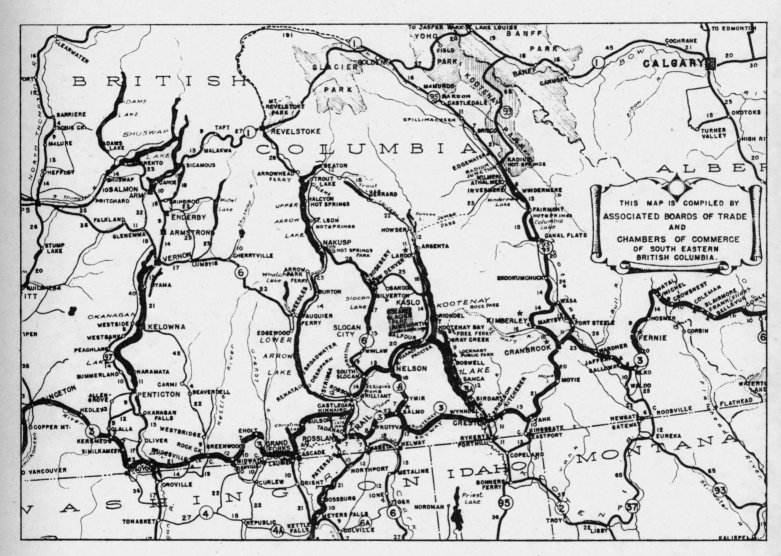

Map of southeastern British Columbia, compiled by the Associated Boards of
Trade.

7

Mining in the Kootenays 1880 ~ 1900

The latter half of the nineteenth century was marked by intensive and world-wide searches for minerals. New technologies based on electricity and oil required huge and unprecedented amounts of iron, lead and copper. Forty years had passed since the first practical commercial demonstration of the telegraph. In Europe and North America tens of thousands of miles of copper wire now connected all the major centers. In the seventies and eighties a world network of submarine telegraph cables had been laid, creating further demands for industrial metals. The first major use of electricity occurred during the nineties in electric traction (tramways and railways) and industrial workshops, creating unheard-of demands for metals.

Also, a long-drawn-out monetary controversy in the United States was over: the advocates of the gold standard (the 'sound money men') had been temporarily defeated by the silverites. The Sherman Silver Purchase Act of 1890 authorized the U.S. Treasury to purchase 4½ million ounces of silver each month at the prevailing market price. Silver prices went to dizzy heights and precipitated a Western U.S. boom in silver mines and mining stock. The country swarmed with prospectors and mining promoters.

Against this background the search for metals spread across the border into the Kootenays. This southeastern region covers some 10,000 square miles of the most mountainous and inaccessible country in the West. Suddenly it was assaulted by prospectors from Idaho and Washington Territory, spilling over the border and up the Kootenay River into Kootenay Lake. The eighties began the great Kootenay mining boom that was to bring this wild uninhabited country into the orbit of Spokane and its businessmen. In the words of Charles St. Barbe in his pamphlet of 1895 on the Kootenay mines, "It is one of Kootenay's advantages that she has a nation of born prospectors close handy (*sic*) just across the border."

Many had known for years that valuable galena deposits of lead and silver lay on the shore of Kootenay Lake. Thrusting out on the east side of the lake was the "Big Ledge," a lump of rock overhanging two tree-covered hills and containing rich veins of silver-lead ore. One hill became the famous **Blue Bell** mine; its ore was so close to the surface that chunks could easily be pried up with a pick in the early days. The outcrop was so prominent that the Indians had long come to the spot to obtain lead for their bullets.

Many myths have grown up around the mine and its discovery. It is said that the botanist David Douglas discovered it in 1825 when he travelled up the Columbia from Fort Vancouver to Fort Colville to explore the country. Though he would have heard about it from the Indians, no record indicates that he went as far as Kootenay Lake. In 1843-44 another botanist, Karl Geyer, was at Fort Colville and later told how Archibald McDonald, Chief Factor of the Hudson's Bay Company in charge of Fort Colville, came to be known as the mine's discoverer.

It is a matter of history that McDonald visited the site and obtained samples of ore. In a letter from Lower Columbia Lake to James Douglas at Fort Vancouver on September 29, 1844, he wrote:

> Some days before I left Colvile (*sic*) I addressed you briefly on the subject of certain ore we talked of; at the same time made up a goodly package of the mineral to go home by the ship for testing in England. I have now to inform you that I myself have since visited that interesting spot and certainly found it pregnant with all that might induce a speedy attempt at working the ore, if any other than mere lead. . . . The west shore . . . presents one of the most splendid views in nature to the eye of the Geologist — every Strata (*sic*) bold, clear, and distinct, & I am much mistaken or they are indications of a very rich mineral country.
>
> By light of a blazing fire which warmed myself & my two naked companions for the night I cut my initials in a large tree alongside of us to commemorate my own dear name and as no nook or corner could be spared me on the recently explored Hyperborian shore; and I do not know but I may yet claim the Kootenais treasure as my own.

Within a month samples of the ore were on their way to London with a covering letter from Chief Factor John McLoughlin to Archibald Barclay, the London secretary of the Hudson's Bay Company:

> I have shipped by the Barque *Columbia* a small box, addressed to you, containing specimens of a mineral found in the vicinity of 'Flat Bow Lake' (now Kootenay Lake) on McGillivray's River

(now Kootenay River) which I lately received from Chief Factor McDonald. . . . From a small portion of the metal tested here, a considerable quantity of very fine soft lead was obtained; but our mode of analysis was not sufficiently accurate to detect the traces of a more precious metal. Silver ore may, notwithstanding, be found associated with the lead in sufficient quantities to make it an object of importance to the Company. . . .

It is not probable that mining operations could be carried on to advantage at Flat Bow Lake, the distance being about 600 miles from the sea coast, and the water navigation so difficult and dangerous that the metal would have to be transported with pack horses more than half the distance by land. The mine is also on the South side of the Columbia River and will therefore in all probability eventually fall within the limits of the United States Territory, and if the reported mineral wealth of that part of the country becomes known to the Americans, it will raise its value and may become an additional motive with their Government to make good their claims. However this may be, I think it only proper that the Governor and Committee should be informed of the fact that we discovered the ore in question and it is with this view the specimens are forwarded.

The specimens went to a London firm of experimental chemists, who reported on April 27, 1847, that "the ore contains sulphuret lead, large proportion Iron (oxide), Lime Silica, alumina."

Further investigation posed serious problems: the low content or non-existence of valuable minerals; the site's inaccessibility; and the conflict of interest with fur trading, the principal commercial objective of the company. So the matter was dropped and for many more years the ore continued to supply lead for the bullets of Indians and the occasional trapper. The mine was certainly known to the pioneers of the gold-rush days. William Fernie, in a letter written long after those days, wrote:

My first knowledge of what is now the Blue Bell mine was in 1865. I was at that time employed as foreman under E. Dewdney Esq. in building the eastern section of the Dewdney trail. I had quit work for the season and arrived in October 1865 at Mr. Dewdney's camp where the trail crosses the river. Mr. Dewdney showed me some galena the Kootenay Indians had brought to him and described the location to him from where the ore was brought. Mr. Dewdney tried to induce me to go and prospect and locate the find. I declined because at that time no mineral lode mined except free gold could be worked to advantage.

The mineral wealth of the Kootenays had to wait upon adequate transportation links. These depended on the decisions of a very few powerful men — James J. Hill from the U.S. Midwest, D.C. Corbin from Spokane, and Van Horne and Shaughnessy from Central Canada. In 1883 the Northern Pacific Railway reached

Sandpoint in Idaho, the southern railhead nearest to the Kootenays. In the north the Canadian Pacific completed its main line by 1886-87. Paddlewheel shallow-draught steamboats were now running down the Columbia from Golden; when the Great Northern arrived at Jennings, Montana, similar vessels would steam northward up the Kootenay to Fort Steele. The developing country in the vicinity of Kootenay Lake was being served by barge and sternwheeler from Bonners Ferry, Idaho.

The Armstrong brothers from Portland, Oregon, were among the first to investigate the region. Primarily steamboat operators, they became interested in development involving silver or lead. A young Cornish prospector of theirs named Thomas Hammill located the Lulu and Hot Springs claims in 1883, the first of many to be staked around Ainsworth. Then he crossed over the lake and did the same thing on the "Big Ledge," which was to become famous as the **Blue Bell** mine. Unfortunately, Robert Evans Sproule (up from Bonners Ferry on a prospecting trip) had also noticed the coloring of the rock on the "Big Ledge" and begun work without registering the claim with the gold commissioner at Wild Horse Creek 100 miles away. There were now two claimants; to settle the dispute the government ordered Edward Kelly, government agent for the Kootenays, to proceed to the spot. Sproule and Hammill had set up separate work camps, and to keep his impartiality the agent ate with the Hammill group and slept in Sproule's camp — keeping a foot in each of the only two camps within 100 miles.

Kelly decided in favor of Sproule. Hammill and his employers appealed the decision to the Supreme Court of British Columbia where it was heard before Chief Justice Matthew Begbie in March 1884. The unpredictable judge reversed Kelly's ruling and ordered Sproule to pay all court costs. Sproule had to part with his claim to meet the costs, which so embittered him that his mind became unbalanced. On June 1, 1885, from a bush near where Hammill was working, Sproule shot him in the back. Hammill died a few hours later while Sproule fled southward, pursued by Constable Henry Anderson of the provincial police and a party of Indians. Anderson posted his party on each side of the Kootenay River not far from the international border. In utter disregard of orders an Indian strayed away from camp to hunt with his gun. Sproule, who had been hiding in the bush for days, heard a shot from what he believed to be a party of Indians, walked into camp and was promptly arrested. He was taken to Victoria and convicted and hanged after a long trial.

Difficulties in development and lack of transportation deterred the Ainsworth syndicate from further work on the **Blue Bell** mine although they had been granted 160 acres of Crown land at Ainsworth and had created a small settlement, the first mining town in the Kootenays.

Attention for the next few years focused on the prospectors. What strange sort of man was this who would suffer hardships in the forests and the mountains, frost-bitten in the winter and tormented by mosquitoes and black flies in the summer, encountering failure after failure year after year? Of those who struck it rich only very few profited from their finds — a life spent in wandering over mountains in faraway places does not prepare a man for sudden unaccustomed fortune. Perhaps to understand it fully the life must be lived. It has certainly produced strong individualists and eccentrics.

The murder of two prospectors (both Americans) by an Indian on the trail between Wild Horse Creek and Golden brought in the police in 1887. Under Superintendent Sam Steele of the Royal North West Mounted Police a post was established at the confluence of the Kootenay and St. Mary rivers to give protection to hundreds of prospectors then roaming the hills.

In the same year, prospectors George Bowerman and George Leyson came up by the Dewdney Trail through Okanagan and Rock Creek to the Rossland area. They worked all summer on a shaft on the southern slope of Deer Park Mountain believing that they had found their fortunes, but 20 feet down they lost the ore, gave up hope and abandoned the claim. But history had been made, for it was the first indication of the Rossland wealth that in a few years was to astound the world.

Two years later Joseph Bourgeois, a notable fur trader and prospector, relocated this find. In the following year it was staked by Oliver Bordeau and Newlin Hoover. It was to become the **Lily May**, the first mine to be developed at Rossland. In March 1890 Bordeau hired Joe Morris to help him do the necessary yearly work to hold

WESTERN MINER

On Red Mountain in the early days. Number 1 shaft, California mine, Rossland, B.C.

127

the claim. After finishing the job there was no money left to pay Joe Morris so he started back to town. On the way he stopped to look at some promising outcroppings and found the **Homestake**, the second oldest mine in the Rossland area. When he reached Nelson he found that he still could not collect his money so he joined Bourgeois in another prospecting expedition. They had noticed red patches on the slope across from Deer Park Mountain and crossed over to examine them. Their findings encouraged them to stake five claims on what turned out to be one of the richest mineralized mountains in the West. Staked on Red Mountain were **Centre Star**, **War Eagle**, **Idaho**, **Virginia** and an extension of **Centre Star** which they called **Le Wise**. (All of them became rich revenue producers.) They hiked back to Nelson to register their claims but found as usual that there was no money. So they persuaded E.S. Topping, deputy mining recorder, to pay the fees, and in return gave him permission to register the extension to the **Centre Star**. Topping paid the $12.50 fee on the **Le Wise** and recorded it under his own name as the **Le Roi**, setting off a chain of events that would rock the financial communities of Spokane and London to their foundations.

A town which grew up below a silver mine— Nelson.

The famous big boulder found 30 miles from Kaslo in 1892. It contained $20,000 worth of silver and lead.

News of the finds on Red Mountain soon became public property and hordes of prospectors poured into the district. At about the same time (1890) silver was found near Ainsworth and a small settlement established at Kaslo. Twenty miles back in the mountains the prospectors reported fabulous finds of rich silver-lead ore. With one pick a miner scratched more than seven tons of ore from the surface and netted himself $900. In the summer of 1891 Eli Carpenter found the **Payne** mine, a future divided producer, and the **Whitewater** — which in just a few years paid its owners $240,000 in profits. Even the cooks in the prospectors' camps shared the good fortune. Paddy McCue, a young Irish lad working as cook for a group of prospectors, found the **Utica** and riches in silver.

The little town of Kaslo, on the west shore of Kootenay Lake about 45 miles north of Nelson, did not have a single settler in 1887. George Thomas Kane, agent for the Sayward Sawmill Co. of Victoria, had selected it as a site for a company sawmill but Sayward turned it down. Kane stayed behind, purchased 8000 acres from the provincial government and floated the Kaslo-Kootenay Land Co. The district and townsite began to boom as prospectors searched the nearby hills and recorded new claims every day. The inhabitants of Kaslo voluntarily banded together to cut a 30-mile trail to the mines, supplemented in the spring of 1893 by a wagon road built by local labor and money.

As usual, progress at the mines was hindered by the difficulties of transportation. Basically the ore went from the mines by pack-horse in summer and rawhide (as explained below) in winter. When it reached the water at Kaslo it was shipped by barge or stern-wheeler down Kootenay Lake to Jennings, Montana, where it was put on railway cars and taken east to the smelters. Superseding the packhorse came the ore wagons with four-horse teams and a load of 7 to 7½ tons of ore. Each round trip would take two days; to lighten the burden some mines installed aerial tramways for part of the distance.

"S.S. Bonnington", built at Nakusp in 1911 and operated by the Canadian Pacific Railroad. She carried prospectors, miners and capitalists for 35 years on the Arrow Lakes and the Columbia River.

The ore was shovelled from the mine into ore cars — sometimes pulled by a horse, more often pushed by a miner — and moved to the outside where it was stockpiled. Then, by pack-train or rawhide, it was taken down the mountain. Rawhiding was the method in winter, when the ore was placed in "raw" cowhides laced up and pulled down the trails by horses. Often the horses did not drag but rode the rawhides down the mountains. On very steep grades the rawhide would slide into the horses' hind legs at which point they would sit back, steer themselves with their front feet and slide down. The horses became so accustomed to their job that they would need no direction from the driver. When the snow

An early way to get the ore to smelters. A rawhide ore train near Sandon, B.C., about 1894.

129

became too deep they would be fitted with wooden snowshoes, or ore sacks filled with brush were tied to their feet.

Kaslo became the distribution point for the mines in the Slocan district and for some years it rivalled Nelson in population. It was, according to Charles St. Barbe, "a thoroughly American mining town . . . a busy bustling place with more saloons than there might be any necessity for." Built at the height of the great silver boom, it had a private bank (one of the very few allowed in B.C.) run by a former governor of the State of Idaho, Col. John M. Burke. When the boom burst the town's prosperity departed as well as its banker.

In 1887 Osmer and Winslow Hall, prospecting brothers from south of the border, found the ore vein of the great **Silver King** mine on Toad Mountain, nine miles from Nelson. The difficulty again was cheap transportation:

> Every ton of ore shipped for reduction has to be packed on mules' backs and carried by wagons over a very rough road at an expense exceeding $30 per ton before it is delivered at the smelting works. Add to this cost of reduction say generally $12 to $15 per ton, only high grade ores will bear the great expense.

So wrote J.M. Kellie, a member of the Provincial Legislature for the Kootenays, in 1891.

Nevertheless, over the years the **Silver King** and other mines on Toad Mountain went into production and a smelter was built at Nelson financed by a British company; its chairman was Sir Joseph Trutch, the first Lieutenant-Governor of B.C.

WESTERN MINER

B.C. MINISTRY OF MINES

In the days of the Kootenay silver boom. Slocan Star mine concentrator at Sandon, B.C.

Blast furnace, Hall Mines smelter, Nelson B.C., 1898. This was the first profitable smelter in B.C.

High among the names of the Kootenay prospectors stands that of the French-Canadian Joseph Bourgeois, co-discoverer of the great mines on Red Mountain. In the East Kootenays, while prospecting around present-day Kimberley, he met some Indians on a berry-picking expedition. They had been looking for the white man's rocks as well as berries and had put both in their containers. But the berries had been plentiful and the stones heavy, so the stones were thrown away. Bourgeois went back, picked up the trail, located the outcroppings and found the **North Star** — a silver-lead mine located near the mineralized mountain now known as the **Sullivan** mine.

The story of the discovery of the great **Sullivan** mine involves Father Coccola, friend of the Indians and grubstaker of many a down-and-out prospector. A party including Pat Sullivan, a tall and handsome Irishman from Bantry Bay, arrived at Fort Steele to try their luck at prospecting. From the reverend father and others they heard accounts of Joe Bourgeois' wonderful discoveries at the **North Star**. Grubstaked by Father Coccola they crossed the ravine from the **North Star** and searched the other side. About one mile from the Bourgeois discovery they staked two claims: the **Shylock** and the **Hamlet**. Little did they realize that they were standing on a mountain of ore. Discouraged, they returned to Fort Steele. With another grubstake from the same source they returned and uncovered a ledge of low-grade lead-zinc ore. They put in four summers' work but they did not have the money to continue; it was left to more powerful organizations to bring the mine into production.

The last of the truly great discoveries came on June 30, 1893, when a Kootenay Indian named Pierre found a great ledge of rock near the shores of Moyie Lake on Yahk Mountain, some 15 miles from the international boundary. He brought a sample of it to Father Coccola explaining that it was a far greater mass of rock than Joe Bourgeois had found.

Father Coccola was a remarkable man. A Frenchman from the island of Corsica, he had been sent out by his order to minister to the Indians of the Kootenays and won their unswerving loyalty and affection. He was keenly interested in the resources of the country and the impact that their development would have on his flock. A standing agreement with his Indians brought all unusual rocks to him. If they were found to be valuable the proceeds would be used within the mission in the service of God and to the Indians' betterment.

The missionary showed the latest find to James Cronin, a mining man with interests in the district, who found it to be high-grade galena. They went to the site and staked two claims: the **St. Eugene** and the **St. Peter**. These became the **St. Eugene** mine, at one time the largest silver-lead producer in Canada. Father Coccola and the Indian Pierre retained a half-interest, sold in the development stages for $12,500. From the proceeds a pretty little church was

In the heart of the Kootenay mining country. An old bridge near Fort Steele.

131

built on the mission grounds — and a comfortable house for Pierre, by then Pierre Cronin.

The discoveries of the southern prospectors from 1886 to 1896 laid the groundwork for all the important mineral developments in that area for the next 70 years. The first silver-lead ores from any southeastern B.C. mine was shipped through Revelstoke in 1887 from a mine on the Illecillewaet. The first ore from the Slocan district left in 1892 by pack-train to Kaslo and boat to Bonners Ferry and then by Great Northern Railway to a Montana reducing works. The **Blue Bell** mine, first seriously worked in 1887, sparked the building of Ainsworth, the first mining town in the Kootenays. The first smelter associated with a producing mine in B.C. was built at Pilot Bay to treat the ore from the **Blue Bell**. The site was chosen in 1891 but building did not actually start until 1894, an indication of the difficulty of promoting smelters in B.C. A year later it started production. Troubles followed, both in the metallurgical process of separating the lead and in obtaining a supply of good smelting coke. Two years later operations were suspended; eventually the buildings and the community disappeared.

COMINCO

Digging footings for the Bluebell mine concentrator at Riondel, B.C., in 1910.

A smelter needs three things: a satisfactory process of separation, an assured supply of ore, and reasonably priced fuel. In these early days neither the metallurgical process nor the quality of coke was satisfactory. It is not surprising that the pioneer smelters appeared along the main line of the C.P.R.

The first was erected at Revelstoke by the Kootenay (B.C.) Smelting and Trading Co., incorporated in London in 1889. It was completed the following year — well equipped with everything imaginable except ore. July 1891 saw it blown in with a few hundred tons of ore from the **Monarch** mine near Field, but the

132

company was unable to obtain any more and the smelter was abandoned the following year.

The second, built at Golden by the Galena Mining & Smelting Co., was sponsored by a group of Calgary men. Completed in 1891, it smelted one carload of ore from the **Monarch** mine and then closed indefinitely. In 1920 the machinery was scrapped and the bricks went to build local homes.

A town which experienced much mining activity with the coming of the railway. Early view of Revelstoke on the Columbia.

B.C. GOVERNMENT

Where railway and sternwheeler met. Site of two early smelters, Golden on the Columbia.

In 1904 another smelter was built at Golden by the Laborers' Co-operative Gold Silver and Copper Mining Co. Using electrical power generated on Hospital Creek, it operated for one evening in the summer of 1905 and then fell silent. In 1937 the property was sold to a speculator at a tax sale and the machinery scrapped. Local opinion held that it had been built as a stock-selling device by a syndicate of mining company promoters.

The mining boom in the Kootenays in the early nineties was not unexpected. Technology in the form of the telegraph, the monthly magazine, the commercial journal and the newspapers, both in Canada and abroad, had heralded the advent of the Kootenays as one of the great mineralized areas of the West.

U.S. capitalists, especially from Spokane, were beginning to show interest in the district. In Spokane, E.S. Topping had interested the money men in the **Le Roi** claim he had acquired so unexpectedly from Joesph Bourgeois, and Daniel C. Corbin had decided to build his railway north. It now ended at Northport some miles from the border but plans were being laid to extend it to Nelson no matter how the legislators felt at Victoria. Another branch would soon connect Northport with Rossland thereby diverting practically all the trade of the Kootenays to Spokane and Washington State.

In the days of steamboating on the Columbia and Kootenay, the Ainsworth syndicate of Portland had applied to Victoria for a charter to produce a railway linking the Arrow Lakes waterways with Nelson and Kootenay Lake. The charter was passed by the provin-

133

cial legislature at Victoria but turned down by the federal cabinet on the grounds that "it would in all probability become a feeder to the Northern Pacific R.R." By the promoters it was seen only as a "portage" line in a water-transportation network extending southward. (The reason behind all this activity was an expectedly heavy traffic in ore from the Kootenay mines to the U.S. smelters.) In 1892 the line was built with the blessing of the B.C. government and under the auspices of the Canadian Pacific Railway.

Three years later the mines above and behind Kaslo became serviced by a 30-mile narrow-gauge line — the Kaslo & Slocan — with the financial backing of the great James J. Hill, a mighty financial power in the U.S. northwest. This gave the Slocan mines access by rail and water to the entire U.S. railway network. An alternative route, supported by the provincial government and built by Canadians, was offered from Slocan Lake westward by way of Nakusp to Revelstoke and the C.P.R. This was also a rail-water route with expensive trans-shipment. On completion of this line (the Nakusp & Slocan) it was leased to the C.P.R. and became integrated into its system. The prime purpose of this feverish railway building was to tap the expanding mineral resources of the Kootenays.

The old Slocan mining town of Sandon, as it appeared recently.

B.C. GOVERNMENT

Top: Western Exploration mill at Silverton in the Slocan district.

WESTERN MINER

Bottom: A little known mining community, Zinctown, some three miles from Whitewater in the East Kootenays, long ago abandoned.

B.C. GOVERNMENT

134

The first commercially successful smelter in B.C. was built at Nelson to treat the ore from the famous **Silver King** mine. The first furnace was blown in January 1896, the second a year later. Unfortunately in five or six years the veins of the **Silver King** began to give out. No new reserves were found.

The smelter operated under difficulties until it was bought by the Consolidated Mining & Smelter Co. in 1912. It was never completely successful as the technological process required a mix of lead-silver ores available from no single mine and only with difficulty from a group of other mines in B.C.

The spotlight now turned to Trail Creek, enjoying a mining boom as spectacular as that of the Rand in faraway South Africa. No B.C. mine more dramatically influenced U.S. and British mining practices and shook the confidence of investors than **Le Roi** on Red Mountain on the outskirts of Rossland.

It has been told how Topping, the deputy mining recorder in Nelson, acquired the claim for a $12.50 registration fee. Samples were obtained from the site and the assay proved so encouraging that Topping left immediately for Fort Colville. He showed the samples to several Spokane lawyers there, and they became ardent salesmen for **Le Roi** and accompanied him by train to Spokane. In a few months Senator W.S. Turner had formed a syndicate amongst his friends which purchased a half-interest from Topping for $16,000. In the summer of 1891 the syndicate conveyed the property to the Le Roi Gold Mining Co., a Spokane-based corporation. Shares were sold locally and many an early purchaser lost his way to an easy fortune by disposing of them as worthless. A Spokane boarding-house keeper took some in payment of a bill

Another recent view of abandoned buildings in the old mining town of Sandon in the Slocan district.

The mines around Rossland in the late 1890's.

F. Augustus Heinze

hopelessly in arrears. A stenographer was handed some to cover a salary long overdue. A tailor took a block in payment for a suit of clothes only under protest, but in four or five years this 'worthless stock' paid more than $1,000,000 in dividends.

Topping returned to Trail Creek, got a Crown grant of 343 acres on the site where the smelter and city of Trail now stand, and set up in the real-estate business.

About this time there appeared at Trail one of the most colorful characters ever to brighten the B.C. mining scene. Frederick Augustus Heinze was an American, born in Brooklyn, to German-Irish parents. At this time 26 years old, shrewd, charming, extremely able and with the soul of a gambler, he surveyed Rossland camp. He made a deal with the owners of the **Le Roi** mine to smelt their ore at a plant yet to be built on the banks of the Columbia near Trail Creek, using 40 acres on the bluff donated by Topping. He also lobbied for and obtained a charter for a railway (the Columbia & Western), an asset of considerable strategic value in the poker-like game now to be played for economic control of the Kootenays. Under this charter he ran a tramway connecting the **Le Roi** mine at Rossland to the Trail smelter.

D.C. Corbin was also building a railway from Red Mountain to connect to his Spokane Falls & Northern across the border at Northport, precipitating a struggle between himself and Heinze for the **Le Roi** ore. It developed into the pattern so familiar today — a struggle to keep Canadian business Canadian. Heinze, though an American, posed as the champion of Canadian rights. It was in his personal interest as well as that of the British Columbians to have the ore from a B.C. mine transported on a Canadian railway to be refined in a Canadian smelter. He took this stand in the Victoria *Colonist* of March 14, 1896, stating that B.C. trade could be virtually independent "if transportation facilities equal to those from the United States are offered." This is what he proposed to do.

A rare picture. The earliest photo known of the start of construction of Frederick Augustus Heinze's smelter at Trail in the autumn of 1895.

136

In contrast, Corbin's personal and corporate interests lay in capturing the Kootenay trade for his railways and bringing it into Spokane. Once his Red Mountain railroad was running he approached the **Le Roi** people with a most attractive offer: he would transport all their ore to Northport just across the border at a reduced rate if they would build a smelter there. The smelter's capital cost would be lower, freed from the heavy Canadian custom duties that Heinze had to pay on machinery to equip the plant. Also, operating costs would be less through the considerable reduction in the cost of bringing in the coke used in the smelting. Heinze had contracted to treat 75,000 tons of **Le Roi** ore at $16 per ton. The cost per ton at Northport with Corbin's help would be only $13.75. The terms were accepted and the Le Roi people chose a site at Northport in Washington State for a smelter with a capacity of 225 tons per day. It came on stream in 1897 with a five-year contract to smelt all **Le Roi** ore.

B.C. MINISTRY OF MINES

The best-known of all the Rossland mines. The compressor plant of the Le Roi mine in 1897.

About the same time Col. I.N. Payton of Spokane, president of **Le Roi**, went to London and arranged a sale with a company promoter there for all the assets of the mine, including the smelter, at a spectacularly inflated price. The promoter, Whittaker Wright, floated a new company (called the British America Corporation) on the London Stock Exchange to take over **Le Roi**. This sale sparked one of the most dramatic episodes in B.C. mining history. A stubborn minority of shareholders in Spokane refused to sell, got an injunction from the U.S. courts forbidding any of the majority shareholders to leave the country with the company seal, and sent deputies to keep them from crossing the line. C.H. MacIntosh, a British America agent, hired a special train in Spokane and instructed the engineer to stop for nothing until he reached Canada. Sheriff Bunce of Spokane held the train crew at gunpoint until the president of the railway intervened and the train began its journey. The sheriff, a lone intruder, rode the coach hanging on to the step

WESTERN MINER

A famous Rossland mine— surface buildings of the War Eagle on Red Mountain.

Portal of tunnel, Le Roi mine, Rossland Mining Museum, Rossland, B.C.

all of the 140 miles to the border, where he was refused entry on the grounds that he carried a deadly weapon. In the following year the minority shareholders finally settled their differences and sold.

This was not the end but just the beginning of the troubles of the **Le Roi**. Wright was the builder of one of the first multi-national business empires. He had mines in Australia, ventures in the Yukon, a finance company in London, and considerable investment in other mines in the Kootenays — all represented in some way by shares on the London Stock Exchange. He had persuaded Lord Dufferin, a former Governor-General of Canada, to act as titular head of his enterprises. Such a name suggested a model of respectability, responsibility and conservatism, but it was misleading. Wright drew glowing pictures of his various ventures by transferring funds and worthless securities from one company to another, and as long as he could manipulate loans around companies not being audited at the time he could keep up appearances. Then in 1899 a sharp drop in the stock market, caused by the outbreak of the Boer War, brought him close to bankruptcy. In December 1900 some essential payments by some of his companies were dishonored through lack of funds and the fat was in the fire.

These financial manipulations had serious effects on the operation of the **Le Roi** mine and smelter. Economies had to be made; mechanical defects became frequent and staff was cut beyond the point of safety. The problem was compounded by the miners' agitation for an eight-hour day and the increasingly militant activities of the union, the Western Federation of Miners. Production fell; the smelter ran into trouble; the profits were drained off by Wright to bolster his other companies. Finally the miners and smelter workers walked off the job.

In October 1901 Whittaker Wright's London & Globe Finance Co. went into bankruptcy. The **Le Roi** mine went the same way on January 2, 1902, owing (amongst other debts) $750,000 to a Canadian bank. In his four years of operation Wright had misappropriated nearly £1,000,000 of profits and capital of the mine to cover losses in his other companies.

A few years later Wright himself was arrested and found guilty of fraud in a celebrated London trial, and committed suicide almost at the foot of the judge who was ready to pronounce sentence.

After a re-organization, improvements were made to the **Le Roi** mine. Then came the problem of amalgamation. The Consolidated Mining & Smelting Co. was trying to acquire producing mines in the Kootenays to assure tonnage for its smelter at Trail. Offers were made to the new directors of **Le Roi**, who with one exception agreed to the terms and signed a five-year contract with the smelter at Trail to treat their ore. The one exception, A.J. MacMillan, was dismissed from his post by his fellow-directors. At the annual meeting the majority of shareholders angrily dismissed the directors, appointed A.J. MacMillan as chief executive and cancelled all agreements with Consolidated. The smelter at Northport was re-opened and intensive development started at the mine. But with better mixes of ores, and the reduction in coke costs by shipment from the Crow's Nest on the Canadian side, smelting at Northport had become uneconomical. In 1911 the **Le Roi** came under the wing of Consolidated and the ore was hoisted through the **Centre Star** shaft and handled through the smelter at Trail. In 1925 large-scale operations were discontinued for good. The mine was virtually worked out.

Up to 1897, as stated by the *B.C. Mining Critic* on May 27 of that year:

> The mines here (B.C.) have been mostly very shallow and the risks have been small compared to what they will be when the depths increase, the workings become more extensive and the employment of more powerful and complicated appliances are rendered necessary.

Lode mining requires large amounts of capital, as costly underground workings demand resources unavailable to single prospectors. Major industrial plants had to be built to crush and process the ore.

The pattern of mining was changing. The increasing use of costly machinery was making U.S. promoters cautious in large-scale development. The individual entrepreneur was being replaced by heavily capitalized companies who sold their shares to a widening clientele of investors in Spokane, London, Toronto or New York. Management of the mines depended on the decisions of groups of investors in faraway places. Miners now had little control over the mines that they discovered or worked in. Thus within a few years mining in the Kootenays became international and big business.

The heavy concentration of capital, miners, mining equipment and transportation facilities in an age of rapid technological change demanded the best in machinery and managerial skills. Use of electricity in industry was in the experimental stage. To transfer electric power 30 miles over a network of wires was almost unheard-of, so it was with skepticism that the people of the Kootenays heard the announcement of a scheme to harness the waters of Bonnington Falls and transmit the resulting electricity to work the machinery in the mines at Rossland. The promoters were not even in the power business but were prominent in local mining and transportation. Patrick A. Largey, president of the Centre Star Mining & Smelting Co., obtained the water rights from the provincial government under his own name and transferred them to a company under his sponsorship. His partners were Oliver Durant, manager of the Canadian Pacific Telegraph Service, and Sir Charles Ross, famous as the inventor and manufacturer of the Ross rifle, the service rifle of the Canadian Army at the outbreak of

A replica of the underground workings of the Le Roi mine, Rossland Mining Museum.

World War I. Construction started in 1898 on a dam and power house at Bonnington Falls, where the Kootenay River plunges 50 feet over a granite cliff. Transmission at 22,400 volts was by a line of cedar poles 30 to 40 feet high. On the same poles four feet below the lower cross-arms were strung the wires of a telephone circuit — the first long-distance telephone line in the B.C. interior.

The whole project was a daring risk, as the art of carrying power over long distances was still in the experimental stage. Even the original insulators had to come from Germany as nobody in North America was in the business of production for such a high voltage. Small cedar roofs tipped the poles to protect the insulators from the weather, giving the appearance of a row of bird houses sprouting in the forest.

Power first flowed over the copper wires in November 1898. The first customers were the city of Rossland (for street lighting) and the six producing mines in the area. The **War Eagle** Mine had already ordered from Montreal the largest mine hoist ever built for electric drive up to that time.

This was the start of the West Kootenay Power & Light which now serves not only industry but the cities and towns of the Okanagan and southeastern B.C. So fast was this new technology perfected and so great was the demand that the original installation had to be enlarged almost at point of completion. New generating machinery was installed in 1899 and in 1907 a new plant was built on the Upper Bonnington Falls with a capacity of 12,000 KW, the largest in the province at that date. It was the mines which made possible twentieth-century technology in an area where twenty years before there had not been a single dwelling.

Down at Trail Creek, Heinze's smelter was facing difficulties by 1897. When Heinze lost the **Le Roi** contract he had problems getting enough ore, and the coke supply was also erratic and expensive. The time had come to find somebody willing to take over what seemed to have become a burden. To the C.P.R., Heinze's railway charter (the Columbia & Western) looked very attractive. Heinze was not free from trouble in his other mining ventures either. In Montana he was locked in deadly legal battles with Marcus Daly and the other copper tycoons of Butte. Circumstances called for both parties to get together. After touchy negotiations with proposal and counter-proposal flying back and forth by telegram between Trail and Montreal, Heinze sold his smelter and the railway and charter to the Canadian Pacific for a reputed $800,000 ($600,000 for the railway and $200,000 for the smelter). Thus Canadian Pacific inherited the role as protector of Canadian business interests against U.S. encroachments.

With the rise of mining in southeastern B.C., demands naturally arose that the ore should be smelted in the locality where it was mined. As has been mentioned, several smelters had already tried

Courthouse at Rossland.

and failed. The problems were immense. Not only were the technological processes of separation unsatisfactory (the science of metallurgy had not yet come up with acceptable solutions), but the fuel situation was alarming. Coke had to be imported from Pennsylvania or Wales at prices that made it almost impossible to smelt in B.C. at a cost that the grade of discovered ores could bear. Enormous coalfields were known to exist in the East Kootenays; this was one of the principal facts that influenced the C.P.R. decision to build the Crow's Nest Pass branch from Lethbridge to Kootenay Lake in 1898.

Under the new federal charter of the Crow's Nest Pass Coal Co., coal mines were opened up at Coal Creek, Michel and Morrissey and a colliery railway built to connect with the C.P.R. The mines lay not far from the town of Fernie and a majority of mine employees lived in the town and commuted daily to work by train.

Beehive coke ovens were built at Fernie and Michel to turn out industrial coke. This was sold to the smelters at Nelson and Trail for about one-half the price of imported coke, at last making the smelters competitive with those across the line. The recovery of coke from the ovens was about 55 per cent of the amount of coal burned, a very disappointing result and well below the average obtained in other coalfields. But because of favorable transportation factors the new product proved a distinct advantage to the struggling smelter industry, especially when the new copper smelters opened in the Boundary country in the first decade of the twentieth century.

Up to 1900 almost the entire output of industrial metals in B.C. had come from the Kootenays. Its mineral wealth became valuable only when the steam railway, that great technological instrument of the nineteenth century, entered the country. The increasing sales of such basic metals as silver, lead and coal to export markets within the space of 20 years peopled southeastern B.C. through a group of small mining towns (Nelson, Kaslo, Rossland) tied together by a network of communications — steamers, wagon roads, railways and telegraph lines. The period laid the foundations of today's mining industry. Before the completion of the C.P.R. main line in 1886-97, the transportation of minerals other than precious metals from B.C. to any market was impossible. With the coming of the railways to the Kootenays, many promising properties there could raise enough funds for development with the assurance of a profitable return on investments.

Once the heart of the biggest mining boom in B.C. history. The city of Rossland as it appears seventy years later.

141

Trail Creek Landing 1890-92. The large building is Hanna's Trail House. Behind it is the hill on which the smelter was built.

8

The Birth of a Great Canadian Enterprise

One of the greatest influences in the fostering of the economy of southeastern B.C. was the birth and growth of the Consolidated Mining & Smelting Co., now known as Cominco. The story, rich in human interest, is that of a great corporation built through the seizing of opportunities by a few brilliant men. Their vision, determination and skills created an enterprise that became an important element in British Columbia life with an influence extending to homes and peoples throughout the Western world.

Soon after 1890 there were hundreds of prospectors and claims in the Rossland-Trail area. Every man was on his own or in partnership with one or two others. Almost none had the capital, technical skills or experience to develop any property efficiently. Among the fortunate few with these assets was Frederick Augustus Heinze, some of whose exploits were described in the previous chapter. Heinze, an early graduate of Columbia University School of Mines, came out to Montana in the nineties and built a smelter at Butte in competition with the copper giants Marcus Daly and Senator William A. Clark. In 1895 he appeared in Rossland and signed a contract to smelt the ore from the newly opened **Le Roi** mine at a plant to be erected on the banks of the Columbia. E.S. Topping, who was working hard to develop a town where Trail Creek flows into the Columbia, donated 40 acres for a site. The smelter began as a small plant with power and heat from steam boilers — and a tramway to the mine at Rossland, a development that was to lead to greater things. Then D.C. Corbin, a Spokane railway promoter, having completed his Red Mountain Railway from Rossland to south of the border at Northport, enticed the **Le Roi** people to build a smelter there. Heinze was stranded. He had a smelter but not enough ore to keep it running. It was fast becoming a white elephant. But he also had something that nobody else in the district (other than D.C. Corbin) had — a railway charter.

In those days the dream of every young aggressive businessman was to own a railway charter with its accompanying land grant. Heinze, knowing where the power lay, had received a charter from the provincial legislature permitting Columbia & Western Railway to build a narrow-gauge road between Trail Creek and Penticton. Furthermore, the route was to be selected by the officials of the company, thus giving Heinze freedom to pick his land. A grant of 10,240 acres of Crown land was to be handed over to the company for every mile of track laid down. If the track was made standard gauge the land grant was increased to 20,000 acres per miles. As an added sweetener the land was not subject to provincial taxation for ten years.

COMINCO

A superb view of the town of Trail and the smelter on the hill in the early 1900's.

Heinze put his tramway from Rossland to Trail under the new concession and waited for buyers. There were two in the field: the Great Northern and the Canadian Pacific. The latter had entered the Kootenays with a line then under construction from Lethbridge to Kootenay Lake. It also owned the short line connecting the Arrow and Kootenay Lakes. Further westward in the Boundary country prospectors had already staked out huge deposits of low-grade copper-bearing ores. The C.P.R. knew all about railway charters and land grants and was not averse to taking risks when the prizes were so alluring. It also knew that James J. Hill and his Great Northern Railway had ambitions in southern B.C.

Sir William Van Horne himself took a trip to Trail to look over the situation and if possible to come to some agreement with Heinze. But Heinze wanted an excessive price and would not sell the railway rights without the smelter. At about the same time Van Horne was introduced to a brilliant mining engineer in his twenties: Walter Hull Aldridge, a contemporary of Heinze and a graduate in

144

the same class from the School of Mines at Columbia University. Aldridge was holding down a good position as manager of the American Smelting & Refining Company's plants in Montana and being wooed by the Guggenheim brothers to join their organization. Then Van Horne suddenly offered him the position of manager of mines for the Canadian Pacific Railway. Though he was reluctant to take it up and came out to Trail only to look over the ground, he was so impressed by the vast mining potential of the Kootenays that he accepted.

COMINCO

Bay Avenue, Trail, in the foreground. The smelter on the hill and, between it and the town, the slag pile.

His first assignment was to complete negotiations with Heinze; this he promptly did, to the satisfaction of the directors in Montreal.

But to gain the greater prize of the charter for $600,000 the C.P.R. had to accept the smelter at an inflated price: the payment of $200,000 was said to be at least $50,000 more than it was worth. The C.P.R. management was not happy with the acquisition of the smelter. The company was in transportation, not in mining, and the smelter had been beset by difficulties in finding materials and man power. It seemed a shaky investment.

Heinze's withdrawal from Rossland mining was viewed in an interesting light by his contemporaries in Butte. Harry C. Freeman in his book *Butte, Montana*, published in 1900, writes of this aspect of Heinze's career:

> A few years ago Mr. Heinze embarked quite extensively upon operations in the Rossland district of British Columbia, but the antagonism of the Canadian Goverment through the instrumentality of subsidized corporations of that country made his efforts extremely hazardous and he retired from the field, but

145

not, however, before he had enhanced his wealth to a most satisfactory extent.

In his new job, Aldridge faced two problems. The first was to make the smelter a useful and economically sound enterprise. The second, intimately tied up with the first, was to find ores in sufficient quantities and of the right quality, ores that could be shipped and processed by the smelter at a profit. This meant tapping all available information on mining activities in Southern B.C. Information on claims being found, on when new mines would come into production and at what tonnage, on the owners of mining properties and their plans, on quantities of ore available — it all had to be gathered. For the first time in B.C., an efficient commercial intelligence network was developed.

Aldridge was writing for information and samples of ore from the Slocan district as early as 1898. D.W. Moore wrote from Kaslo on March 22 of that year:

> The Payne mine will ship 60 tons daily. They could ship more but are only working with a staff of 75 men. Their output could be increased to 100 tons daily if they wished. All the other mines will not account for 1,000 tons from March 22, 1898, to July 1st.

In the spring of 1901 Aldridge commissioned John Redman, a consulting engineer in Kamloops to report on the local mines. On June 15, 1901, Redman reported on the **March** mine on Kamloops Lake, "The mine is 3 miles from the railway and is a very desirable smelting ore." There were half-a-dozen promising mining prospects and "all the ores are of a cheap smelting nature and very desirable I imagine to run with the Rossland ores."

One of the results of this network of commercial intelligence was a vast accumulation of facts on all aspects of mining in B.C., something possessed by no other mining man or organization. Much of the information was fed back to Sir Thomas Shaughnessy and other senior members of C.P.R. management in Montreal. It enabled them to make some very shrewd decisions about railway expansion in Southern B.C. When the time came to support Aldridge and his team in the formation of the Consolidated Mining & Smelting Co., the information was already in Montreal and working for them.

Under great pressure, management had put a considerable sum of money into the purchase of the Trail smelter. It was now reorganized under a new title — the Canadian Smelting Works. Aldridge's first task in the spring of 1898 was to close down the operation and re-design and re-equip the smelter at a cost of $100,000. New copper furnaces and roasting ovens were installed. The steam boilers were taken out and a connection made with the new Bonnington Falls-Rossland electric transmission line of West Kootenay Power.

146

To the directors of the C.P.R. the purchase of Heinze's smelter seemed to be a highly speculative venture. Not only was it over-hauled, but the **Le Roi** mine had pulled out and taken away the largest tonnage in the Rossland area. Both the Rossland mines and those in the Slocan district were in the process of development — they had very little ore on hand and even less to ship. Aldridge tried to contract for large tonnages from the recently discovered copper deposits at Phoenix and Greenwood in the Boundary country, but these sites were not yet ready for extensive mining. The low grade of the ores and the long haul made them uncompeti-tive. In the end Boundary ores were treated in Boundary smelters and the Trail refinery was effectively cut off from this productive region. The only tonnage obtained was from a leased C.P.R. mine (the **Snowshoe**) at Phoenix at an unprofitable rate; its main value to Trail was that of providing a good smelting flux. The Rossland miners strike of 1901 completely closed the smelter as all deliveries of ore ceased. Novel solutions had to be found to meet a serious problem.

COMINCO

Bay Avenue, Trail, looking towards the smelter, pre-World War I.

Thanks to Aldridge's efforts in spreading the right word among the decision-makers in Montreal and Ottawa, the federal government in 1901 granted to Canadian smelter operators a bounty on lead re-fined in their refineries. This made it profitable for the first time for the silver-lead ores of the Slocan to be refined in Canada. To take advantage of this opportunity two lead furnaces were installed at Trail. They offered only a partial solution, for the bullion still had to be sent to Tacoma for final processing; the contract, though, did specify that it had to be carried as far as practical over Canadian Pacific lines.

How could the smelter be kept busy? Aldridge found the solution with a master-stroke. A new industry — lead refining — came into being in British Columbia. The method by which this was accom-plished set a pattern of research orientation that still characterizes the management of the company.

Dr. A.G. Betts of Troy, New York, had been experimenting in a new method of lead extraction by an electrolytic process, and Aldridge purchased the Canadian rights to the Betts patent. He then com-missioned Betts to design and supervise the erection of the first commercial application of the process at the Trail smelter. In October 1902, from the New York Grand Union Hotel, Dr. Betts submitted an estimate for a 50-ton lead refinery; the cost would be $156,500, later reduced by early exercises in cost control to $121,900.

The refinery was the first of its kind in the world and created a furor in metallurgical circles. Japanese engineers came to see it in operation and requests for details came from such unlikely mining places as Barcelona, Spain. Initial equipment consisted of 240 asphalt-lined wooden cells housed in a frame building with a rated capacity of 10 tons per day. The cells continued in service until

147

1914 when they were replaced by concrete ones. The basic principles of the Betts process remained unchanged for 50 years and were used in many lands. At Trail constant improvement and changes in the equipment steadily increased the daily output. The venture proved itself within a year. By February 1904, Aldridge was reporting exultantly to Sir Thomas Shaughnessy, "We now control the supply and price of pig lead throughout Canada as well as in China and Japan."

Aldridge also proposed to put in a pipe-making machine and a rolling machine at Trail to turn out lead pipe and sheets of lead. "There is no reason," he wrote to Shaughnessy, "why we should ship pig lead to Montreal, have it manufactured there and returned to Winnipeg and Western points in the form of pipe and sheet."

In reply, Shaughnessy brought out clearly the limitations under which Aldridge had to work in building up an industrial complex in B.C.:

> I should be very glad indeed (Shaughnessy wrote) to see corroding works established on a good sound basis, but this company will not invest more money in this direction. We have gone rather further than we should in providing refinery works and that must be considered the limit of our investment.

Zinc in the lead ores was a particularly bothersome problem. Ores with a high percentage of zinc could not be refined by any economical method then in commercial use and therefore were of little value. In 1903 Aldridge made searching inquiries into the possibility that the Canadian Smelting Works or some other interested agency might set up a zinc refinery. The Trail smelter sent 1500 lbs. of Kootenay ores to Wethrill Separating Co. of Newark, N.J., to see if they could find ways of extracting the zinc in the hope that such a process could be set up at Trail. But Aldridge was ahead of his time — the problem continued to plague him for another twelve years.

Under Aldridge's able management the Trail smelter became the most aggressive and competitive of all Kootenay operations. It drew its ores from the mines of Rossland, Slocan and Lardeau districts and from the **St. Eugene** at Moyie. It finally forced its chief competitor, the Hall smelter at Nelson, to close — but not before Aldridge had made a dramatic and puzzling move. He had long been friends with J.C.S. Fraser, the manager of the Bank of Montreal at Rossland, who had helped to complete arrangements with Heinze. The bank held a large overdraft against the smelter at Nelson. When fears were expressed that the overdraft would not be paid, Aldridge released S.G. Blaylock, one of his ablest assistants and the man who one day would head all the consolidated companies, to take charge at Nelson and see that the bank got its money back. The only mines that Trail could not reach were the low-grade copper ones in the Boundary country, where copper

Inside the lead refinery. Trail smelter, about 1917.

148

smelters had been built to service them exclusively.

In 1905, one of the better years, the lead smelter was in a particularly strong position. Through the concerted efforts of the Associated Boards of Trade of Southeastern B.C. and the Lead Miners & Smelters of British Columbia, the lead bounty (now paid to the mine owners and not to the smelters) had been extended until 1908. There were still no signs of exhaustion of ore at the **St. Eugene** mine near Moyie, the largest supplier of lead-enriched ore to Trail. In contrast, the mines at Rossland showed little promise. The very efficient and low-cost copper smelting operations in the Boundary country had adversely effected the copper furnaces at Trail. The situation was becoming critical.

Aldridge, who had sized up the situation a year before, had been quietly forming a group mainly within the C.P.R. management to buy up and consolidate some of the principal mines. In this endeavor he was supported by Edward Beatty (future president of the C.P.R. and at the time in its legal department) and the ubiquitous Mr. Fraser of the Bank of Montreal at Rossland. The time seemed ripe for a change in ownership. George Gooderham of Toronto, a partner in the **War Eagle** and **Centre Star** (two of Rossland's premier mines) and the **St. Eugene** at Moyie, was in failing health. He died in 1905. After months of negotiations in which Edward Beatty employed all his skills as a lawyer and negotiator, the C.P.R. interests bought out the partnership and took over at Rossland. Aldridge persuaded Pat Stewart to forsake coal mining at Bankhead and take charge. His great technical knowledge and energy soon revealed unsuspected ore bodies in the Rossland mines. Production and ore reserves increased substantially.

At the same time the **St. Eugene** mine and the Canadian Smelting Works were evaluated, and talks began to find ways to consolidate the mines at Rossland and Moyie with the Trail smelter. The management of the **Le Roi** mine was also invited to participate.

It was said that James Cronin, the man who had pioneered the **St. Eugene** and was now manager, mined and shipped in those difficult days only the higher grade ores and so increased monthly profits. The stock market awoke to this fact and shares tripled in value. In the final agreement of consolidation **St. Eugene** received a larger share of the new company stock than the engineers had estimated in their professional reports.

Out of all this emerged, in 1906, the biggest mining corporation yet seen in the Kootenays — the Canadian Consolidated Mines — with 1000 employees and a small but successful smelter at Trail. In a few months the name was changed to the Consolidated Mining & Smelting Company of Canada. Its creators were at the very heart of Canadian commercial and financial power. The president, W.D. Matthews, was ranked by the *Montreal Standard* among the 23 men who controlled the Canadian economy at the time. Aldridge became managing director at Trail. The Canadian Pacific Railway sat in the driver's seat with slightly over 54 per cent of the stock — practically the same as its holdings today.

Thus the Consolidated Mining & Smelting Company was born into the Canadian financial establishment. Its motivating philosophy, as relevant today as it was 70 years ago, was well expressed by Aldridge:

> The Consolidated Mining & Smelting Company of Canada is not dependent upon a single mine nor upon any single mining district, but its interests and business besides being to an extent industrial will also be so diversified as to minimize as far as possible the speculative element.

Although at that time Cominco appeared in the North American context only as a small mining and smelting company, little different from a number of others, its formation practically ended serious U.S. competition in the Kootenays except in coal. It was the final step in the 25-year struggle to keep the Kootenays within the Canadian economy.

COMINCO

At the time of the formation of the Consolidated Mining & Smelting Co. Trail smelter as it looked in 1906.

When this group of producing mines and a smelter came under the umbrella of Canada's greatest transportation system it was only the beginning of Consolidated's long road to domination in southeastern B.C. To protect the position of the smelter at Trail, the company had to be sure of adequate supplies of ore of the right mix so that the metallurgical processes installed in the plant could handle it. The mines had to become more efficient and further reserves of ore had to be found.

On the Rossland scene, Pat Stewart put new life into the **War Eagle** and **Centre Star** with brilliant development work that produced shipments of 1,000 tons per day to the smelter. At **St. Eugene**, mainstay of the lead smelter, mining was now being done at the top of the hill and the ore hauled down to the concentrator by aerial tramway. The mine saw its best years in 1907-08, when the work force was increased and improved mining machinery was brought in. The little town of Moyie boasted 500 souls and six hotels and was an orderly law-abiding place. Gone were the boom days, the image of a Western frontier mining camp. In February 1908, when S.G. Blaylock took over management, everything appeared normal — the mine, it seemed, would last another dozen years or more. But the next year's exploration and development work on the property almost drew a blank. Production fell almost by half. The mine appeared to be on the point of exhaustion.

Nobody in management or outside had any premonition of the sudden **St. Eugene** collapse. Insistent demands came from Trail for more of the lead ores and engineers were forced to look very hard at other properties. Some of the most astute people in the business had looked at the **Sullivan** mine, now owned by the Guggenheims of New York through one of their subsidiaries. Despite many efforts, no one up to this point had arrived at a satisfactory solution to the problem of the separation of the **Sullivan** ores. It was not by choice but through necessity that Consolidated became involved in the **Sullivan**.

The story of the finding of this great mine has been told in the previous chapter. Three of the four original partners (Pat Sullivan had been killed in the Coeur d'Alene district of Idaho in the winter of 1892) worked their claims intermittently from 1892 to 1896. In the latter year they sold out for $24,000 to a group of Spokane men who operated under the name of the Sullivan Group and were also interested in the famous **Le Roi** at Rossland. The group began shipping ore to Trail and Nelson but the smelters charged high penalties for the zinc content and little profit was realized. Like many others they thought that they could do better themselves, so in 1903 they built a smelter at Marysville, a little settlement south of Kimberley on the C.P.R. track. Here they encountered the usual problems associated with Sullivan ore. One of the pioneer workers in that smelter described their plight:

> We were frozen up most of the time. The zinc would cause a crust to form in the furnace and soon a whole charge would solidify. Sometimes it would take months to get the operation going. Then it would freeze up again. It was hopeless.

Plagued by such metallurgical and financial problems the whole operation closed down in 1907 and the Sullivan Group soon went bankrupt. In 1909 its holdings were purchased by the Federal Mining and Smelting Co., a Guggenheim corporation. Around that time Aldridge instructed Pat Steward, Consolidated's manager of mines, and S.G. Blaylock, superintendent of **St. Eugene**, to examine it in their usual careful way. Like everyone else, they were struck by the immense amount of mineralized rock. They sensed the great potential almost by instinct, and concluded that small-scale selective mining could make it pay. More effective ways could, in time, be found to treat the difficult ores. In fact, they had very little choice: Trail was desperate for ore and this was the only likely source of further supplies. A limited tonnage of high-grade material could be hand-picked and sent by C.P.R. to the smelter. They did not realize that **Sullivan** ore would give Consolidated the firm foundation for its phenomenal success in future years. On their recommendation the company took up an option on the property in December 1909.

COMINCO

The first smelter built to exclusively treat Sullivan ore. Marysville smelter in its working days.

A research program was soon mounted to overcome the problems of separation of the **Sullivan** ores. The concentrators of the **Le Roi** at Rossland and the **Highland** at Ainsworth were used for test work. At **St. Eugene,** where the mine had been completely closed, the mill was remodelled for this particular job. These experimental mills used every method in the book: water concentration, air jigs, flotation, direct fusion of metals, efforts to volatilize the metals by mixing them with coal or coke dust and heating in revolving kilns. Leaching was then tried; in 1914 toasting, leaching and electrolysing proved successful in extracting the zinc, but at a cost greater

152

than the normal markets would bear. Finally, in 1920, largely through the efforts of R.W. Diamond, the problem became solved by the differential flotation process and the **Sullivan** mine became the brightest jewel in the Consolidated mineral treasury. This research program extending over a period of ten years was unparalleled in Canadian industry and became a classic of industrial research.

In 1911 W.H. Aldridge resigned to take a better position with a big New York mining organization. He was given the job of co-ordinating the mining interests of the Thompson group of Wall Street. It was an amicable parting and for many more years he continued as a director of Consolidated, constantly writing to and feeding back mining information to his friends in the company and maintaining an impact on the Kootenay mining scene.

Even before Van Horne hired him he was an experienced chemist, metallurgist and assayer. Coupled with these talents Aldridge possessed ability as an organizer, administrator and businessman. Like all great leaders he had the ability to pick talented men and hold their loyalty to himself and the company he represented. The men that he gathered around him — Turnbull, Stewart, Blaylock — became in their turn leaders in the company and built Consolidated Mining & Smelting to heights never dreamed of by its founders.

S.G. Blaylock is typical of the group. A clergyman's son, he was born in 1879 and educated at Bishop's College in Lennoxville, Quebec. He graduated from McGill with a Bachelor of Science degree in mining and metallurgy in 1899. In that year he came west and was hired by Aldridge as assayer in the Canadian Smelting Works at Trail. He was a large man with the build of an athlete, much given in those days to sport and to tennis in particular.

Blaylock became one of Aldridge's commercial intelligence team, analysing the ores as they came from the different mines and reporting on their acceptability. He went to the Hall smelter at Nelson in 1907 as superintendent, but when economic forces outside his control compelled it to shut down he returned to Consolidated as superintendent at **St. Eugene**. Once the ore gave out there the company transferred him to the **Sullivan** mine as boss. He stayed there until R.H. Stewart became general manager of the company in 1911, when he came back to Trail as his right-hand man. He was modest by nature. On receiving the James Douglas Medal of the American Institute of Mining and Metallurgical Engineers "for his development of the selective flotation process for the lead-zinc-iron ores . . . (essential) in solving the problems necessary for the treatment of the ores from the **Sullivan** mine," he was asked to identify the most important factor in this triumph. He replied, "It has been the co-operation of the entire staff. . . working for a common end."

Aldridge introduced two concepts that were new to the industry

COMINCO

A great force in the affairs of the Consolidated Mining & Smelting Company, and a leading figure in the development of the selective flotation process for Sullivan ore— S.G. Blaylock.

153

and to the business practices of the day — research and teamwork.

The first and possibly the more influential was the concept of industrial research, practically unknown to Canadian business until after the first decade of the twentieth century. It was somehow connected with unusual and eccentric people, cranks and inventors and absent-minded professors of the physical sciences. The commercial pioneering of the Betts lead refining process gave the Canadian Smelting Works a monopoly in the national lead industry and created a new activity for Canadian business. By diligent efforts in Canada and Great Britain, Aldridge uncovered the advantages of the little-known Huntington-Heberlein roasting process of de-sulphurizing ores, thereby avoiding most of the problems of furnace crusting. By 1909 the Trail smelter was the only plant in Canada west of Kingston producing lead bullion. It was simply the reluctance of the C.P.R. head office that prevented the establishment of a lead fabricating and manufacturing industry in British Columbia.

Underground at the Sullivan mine at the turn of the century.

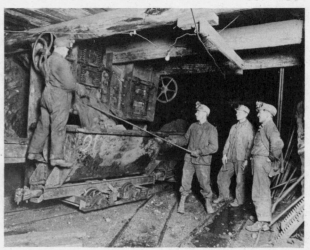

Pulling ore from a chute, Sullivan mine, pre-World War I.

In the field of industrial pollution control, Aldridge was acquiring information as early as 1908 — looking into the problems of treating the gases as they emerged into the air from the ore-reducing furnaces "in a manner that will not be objectionable to people living in the area." (This enlightened view was contrary to those expressed by the editor of the *Trail Creek News* when he wrote, "The thicker the smoke ascending into the skies from Smelter Hill the greater is Trail's prosperity. This is what Trail people like to see.")

He initiated an extensive correspondence with both H.B. Underhill, president of the Selby Smelting and Lead Co. of San Francisco, and Dr. J.G. Davidson of McGill University College in Vancouver on a process then being experimentally tested at the Selby smelter to recover sulphuric acid from the smoke emission of the smelter chimneys.

Dr. Davidson, through the company which he represented, offered to put in recovery equipment at Trail but Consolidated refused (in a letter of June 6, 1908) on the grounds that the installations could not be justified unless the process could make commercial sulphuric acid.

In this approach Aldridge was 25 years ahead of his time; the sulphur recovery plant installed by Consolidated in 1931 not only revitalized farming around Trail, but was the basis of the company's fertilizer industry.

The second innovation was that of teamwork. Talented, college-trained young people were attracted to Aldridge. He gave them opportunities that no other organization in the Kootenays could offer. The result was a team of technically proficient people who worked together for the common good of the company and not for their own reputation or personal advantage. Teamwork was little understood and seldom practiced in the Canadian commercial world of that day. It produced high morale and an ability to tackle problems that had baffled some of the best brains in the industry. The ultimate triumph of his managerial skills was his legacy of a group of able managers that carried the company over many difficulties for many years.

Under the direction of R.H. Stewart, ore shortages and some of the problems related to the **Sullivan** mine were gradually solved. As **St. Eugene** faded out, the **Centre Star** mines became the leading ore suppliers for the Trail smelter. Their rehabilitation had not been easy. Much exploration and development work had to be done before promising new ore bodies were discovered; new mining methods, better machinery and teamwork created a new highly efficient operation. Right up to 1914 the **Centre Star** group supplied the largest tonnage to the smelter.

The **Sullivan** was still beset with problems. Consolidated had moved in when all the others had abandoned it, leasing it in 1909 and taking up an option to purchase in 1910. It was not until 1913 that Consolidated became absolute owner. In the meantime, selective mining produced lead ore with an acceptable zinc content and hand-sorted high-lead-zinc ore for shipment to Trail. The annual tonnage in 1910 was only 23,000 tons — far less than the 175,000 shipped by **Centre Star**. The low grade of the ore and its heavy zinc content presented a very difficult situation. In 1910 solution of the **Sullivan** ore's smelting problem became a prime activity in the company. Four years later an experimental process of zinc extraction by an electrolytic method was worked out. A one-ton testing mill was set up at Trail, but costs of zinc extraction were prohibitive. It was mothballed.

One of the many mines dependent on the Trail smelter for the final processing of its ore. The Whitewater at Retallack, Slocan district.

155

Then World War I broke out and the framework of normal trade seemed suddenly to have crumbled. On August 4, 1914, all payments by Trail on silver and lead accounts were suspended because of the demoralization of the markets.

The smelter tried to get its custom shippers to finance their own ores up to the point when the metal was sold. Many mines could not stand these abnormal conditions and closed down.

COMINCO

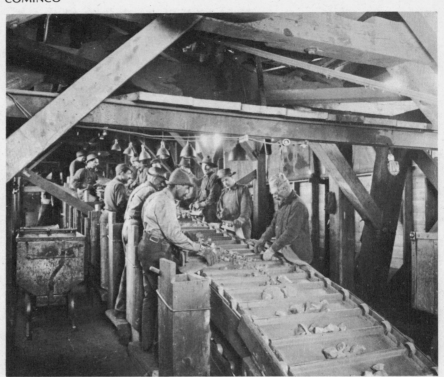

Handsorting Sullivan ore, 1909.

In the spring of 1915, a brighter outlook was seen for the silver and lead markets, while demand skyrocketed for all metals used in munition production. At the request of the Shell committee of the Canadian government, Consolidated agreed to erect a pioneer electrolytic zinc-refining plant. When the Imperial Munitions Board came into being the agreement was supported by a firm sales contract to take all production of zinc for the British war effort. Consolidated designed the new plant with a capacity of 30 tons of zinc per day and put up the first steel for construction in October 1915. As stated in *Industrial Progress*: "The completion of this new plant will mean that practically a new industry will be added to the wealth producing capacity of this district."

Once again opportunity had knocked and Consolidated was ready and responded. It was the first commercial electrolytic zinc refinery in Canada.

The prosperity and continued expansion of Consolidation rested upon four foundations: men, mines, smelters and cheap electric power. It has been told how the first three were built. For the fourth the company had to depend during the first ten years on an outside source. The previous chapter described how West Kootenay Power & Light was organized to supply the Rossland mines with electricity. Initially the Trail smelter was not a customer but the C.P.R. later tapped the Bonnington-Rossland power line. As the capacity of the lead smelter increased, so did its power requirements. Partly because of this and partly because of the burgeoning mines and smelters in the Boundary country, a new 16,000 H.P. plant was built at the Upper Bonnington Falls. It housed two turbines delivering 8000 H.P. each to a pair of Canadian General Electric generators. Activated in 1907, the power was transmitted by a 60,000 volt line as far west as Greenwood.

Built into the scheme was an unharnessed future capacity of another 16,000 H.P. This is probably one of the reasons why the C.P.R. directors in 1908 initiated studies for the electrification of the railway from Nelson to Greenwood, a massive job far ahead of its time in Western Canada.

Electricity was to be supplied by West Kootenay Power. The plans were never carried into operation but it showed how closely the mines and smelters of Southern B.C. were tied to advances in technology.

Additions were not made to the West Kootenays' generating capacity until 1914, when a third turbine was installed at the Upper Bonnington plant. Wartime demands at Trail, especially the new zinc refinery, prompted a fourth and last turbine by 1916. But this was not enough. Wartime restrictions and the difficulties of financing expansion put a stop to any further development by West Kootenay Power. Sir Charles Ross, the principal shareholder in the company, was going through a trying time in a national controversy concerning the Ross rifle, so the idea that Consolidated buy a controlling interest met with a favorable response. It was of advantage to Consolidated to get control of its sources of power; in an unprecedented move in 1916 it bought all the common shares of West Kootenay Power & Light. Thus the fourth foundation was added to the Consolidated corporate structure, making it one of the first integrated companies in Canada and the dominant voice in business in the Kootenays.

Throughout all these years the guiding genius of West Kootenay Power had been Lorne Campbell. He was one of the most colorful personalities that the Kootenays ever produced. Born and educated in Perth, Scotland, he came to Canada as a youth to seek his fortune and joined the engineering staff of the Edison General Electric in Toronto in 1889. He came west in 1898 as the manufacturer's representative in the installation of the first power house at Bonnington Falls, and stayed in B.C. as general manager of West Kootenay Power.

COMINCO

Portal , Sullivan mine.

He was a man of strong and authoritarian character, and West Kootenay Power became an instrument of his personality. On many occasions he and Aldridge clashed. Once in the early years, when the smelter had closed down for a few weeks, West Kootenay sent in its usual bill for services rendered. Aldridge complained bitterly that the charges were too high, that as the smelter was closed no power had been used. Campbell retorted that the smelter had to pay whether it worked or not. "Furthermore," he added. "if you do not pay this bill we will cut you off." Aldridge had no choice.

Campbell was more strong-willed than many around him, even though the period was marked by businessmen who ran their concerns in individualistic ways. This possibly was a major asset to a small company pioneering a new business in a new country. The company that he headed for so many years not only provided industrial power for the building of the mining and smelting industry in Southern B.C., but helped materially in making life more liveable for the workers. It opened its first retail store in Rossland in 1899 to rent and sell electrical home appliances. The cost of running each vacuum cleaner by the City of Trail added 50 cents per month to its light bill. An electric iron in the home cost $1.43 per month. The streets of mining towns which ten years before had not even existed were now lit by electric lamps. Business establishments, public buildings, restaurants, and saloons could now be used after dark without the aid of smoky oil lamps. West Kootenay Power brought the camps and mines and towns of the Kootenays into the modern age.

Underground tramway station, Sullivan mine.

COMINCO

GREENWOOD SMELTER

In this wilderness of rugged mountains, ore was first found in the late 1880's. Further prospects led to the building of a large smelter by the B. C. Copper Co. From 1901, copper, gold, and silver poured from its furnaces. Fed by the great Motherlode Mine, it employed 400 men. The collapse of inflated war-time copper prices forced closure in 1918.

DEPARTMENT OF RECREATION & CONSERVATION

To commemorate the passing of an era. The Boundary country's copper smelters, of which Greenwood was one, built up a great industry from copper ore, employing thousands.

9

Where Copper is King

Some 40 or 50 miles west of Rossland lies the Boundary country, a district along the Canadian-U.S. border between the valleys of the North Fork of the Kettle River and Boundary Creek. In the gold-rush days of the 1860's placer gold had been found along Boundary Creek, but for the next 20 years there was no further mining activity. Then prospector James McConnell staked a claim on Rock Creek a few miles above Kettle River. In 1887 David Leyson and George Bowerman, a team that staked and worked the first claim near Rossland in the same year, located the **Big Copper** near the future **Mother Lode** mine in Deadwood Camp. This claim was never worked by them and lapsed. Two other prospectors, Ed Lefevre and James Lynch staked the **King Solomon** in the same area; they promptly sold it to D.C. Corbin, a Spokane railway tycoon who was the first prominent financier to invest in Boundary copper.

The biggest finds came in 1891, when William McCormack and Richard Thompson staked the **Mother Lode** in Deadwood Camp. Phoenix produced the big discoveries: gigantic ore bodies contained in the **Old Ironsides** and **Knob Hill** claims by Matthew Hotter and his partner, Henry White. Nearby locations were soon staked.

It was one thing to locate these vast deposits of low-grade copper ore, but quite another to find moneyed people willing to risk their capital in purchasing and developing them. The Rossland and Slocan booms were on — mining men preferred to risk money there, rather than on the low-grade ores of the Boundary country. After all, the nearest railway was south of the border in Washington State 75 miles away; no wagon roads or trails existed in the region and freight charges were prohibitive.

Howard C. Walter, a mining man from Spokane, came in around 1892 and acquired a number of high-grade claims at practically no cost to himself. Prospectors no longer had faith in such ore finds and viewed the grade as too low to be worth the trouble. Walter brought in two stamp mills for Boundary Falls and sent a few shipments by mule to the Everett smelter. Then came the slump of 1893. Metal prices declined and the Boundary country became practically deserted.

Undaunted, Henry White interested P.J. Graves, an electric railway magnate of Spokane, in the **Old Ironsides** claim. Graves took a half share and started development in a small way in 1895-96. After a few months, though, his Spokane backers refused to advance any more money. Ore tests showed a copper recovery well below the smelter charges of $8 per ton. The Northport smelter declined to take payment for its work, explaining that it was "not customary for smelters to demand charges for payment of ore when same is less than their usual treatment charges because they don't have to smelt the ore unless they want to."

The beginnings of Phoenix, 1900.

The town of Phoenix in its heyday, with one of the mines in the background.

Graves managed to find new investors in Canada (S.H.C. Miner of Granby and his associates in Quebec's Eastern Townships) and undertook systematic development. A steam power plant was installed after being carted over 65 miles of poor wagon road from the nearest railhead in Washington State — at a haulage cost that almost doubled the price of the machinery. An air compressor to drive a battery of power drills arrived by the same route.

But how should the ore be processed? Its grade was too low and transportation costs too high to justify shipping it out to any smelter beyond the Boundary country. Grand Forks, at the junction of the Kettle River and its North Fork, was chosen as the site for the region's first smelter. The 'Granby smelter' may well have been the only one that was ever built on the proceeds of the sale of town lots. The Miner-Graves Syndicate was a large owner of land in and around Phoenix, the settlement that grew up to service the surrounding mines. Just before the turn of the century, much of the property went up for sale as town lots. Prospective bidders came in from hundreds of miles around, only to find all the lots sold. Prices ran from $500 to $600 — a goodly sum in those days — and by the end of the sale the syndicate found itself richer by $100,000. The furnaces first blew on August 13, 1900, just one month after the first ore train had left the mine site at Phoenix for Grand Forks.

Neither the development of the mines nor the building of the smelter would have been possible without the coming of the railway. The Columbia & Western (a C.P.R. subsidiary) reached Midway via Grand Forks in 1899, giving the Boundary district a through rail connection with the East Kootenay coalfields and Central Canada. Its building was not without international interest as the planner was the famous U.S. engineer John F. Stevens, who later won world fame as chief engineer in the building of the Panama Canal. The C.P.R. built a spur to the mines at Phoenix and soon was carrying 700 tons of ore daily to the smelter. In 1901 the rate increased to 1400 tons; by 1904 it was 2000; the peak figure of 4500 tons per day

GRANBY MINING COMPANY

What it looked like after Granby left in 1919. An open pit copper mine at Phoenix.

Another view of one of the Granby open pit copper mines at Phoenix.

in 1918 marked the largest copper operation of its time in the British Empire. By the end of 1917, 15 million tons of ore had been carried from the Phoenix mines — a colossal tonnage.

The settlement around the mines was fast growing into a town with all the modern conveniences that could be expected. In its heyday Phoenix served as a base for several mining companies other than Granby. B.C. Copper, Dominion Copper, and the **Snowshoe** mines all had nearby properties. Served by two railways — the C.P.R. and the Great Northern — Phoenix enjoyed the benefits of telephones, electric light, and a domestic water system. Recreational facilities included curling and skating rinks, and 17 saloons operating around the clock.

Like the Consolidated Mining & Smelting Co. at Trail a few years later, Graves and Miner soon saw the benefit of bringing into one organization all their individual enterprises in the Boundary country. Thus was born the Granby Consolidated Mining & Smelting Co., an amalgamation of their interests in mineral claims, real

163

A close-up of the Granby ore car designed by Frank Knott and built in the company's shops at Grand Forks.

estate, mines, and smelting works. The creation of one corporate structure, finally accomplished in 1902, tightened up administration and eased the problems of raising money.

Granby's high-volume operation, through labor-saving devices, achieved economies that were the admiration of the mining fraternity.

"I was really surprised," said John Stanton of New York, a director of **Granby** and a leader in the U.S. copper industry, "to see so intelligent and up-to-date a company in operation. . . . I refer especially to mining methods, the mining and smelting plants and system of bookkeeping." That was in 1903. In January 1904, the *Phoenix Pioneer* wrote: "The necessity of saving every few cents possible on each ton of ore sent to the smelter on account of low grade has brought economies that have heretofore been unthought of in the history of mining in this province."

The greatest railway disaster in Phoenix' history. The wreck of the Canadian Pacific Railroad ore train on August 23, 1904, when it ran wild down Phoenix Hill.

Aerial view of one of the copper mines at Phoenix, run by Granby Consolidated.

There was continuous expansion. The end of 1903 saw six blast furnaces in operation; by 1905 the total had grown to eight, housed in the largest copper smelter in the British Empire. Of the labor-saving machinery that was invented on the premises, the best known was the **Granby** ore car. Frank Knott's design led to a steel side-dumping car with a capacity of (at first) three tons, easily and cheaply manufactured in the company's machine shops. It became standard equipment in the industry.

Another innovation was a drill-sharpening machine that eliminated the need for many blacksmiths and forges. The design, by head blacksmith Martin McHale, was taken over by the machine-tool industry and modified versions were sold to mining and exploration companies. Superintendent Hodges of the smelter designed and produced an automatic furnace charger that greatly reduced the time and manual labor for this operation. Much of this heavy equipment was manufactured in the **Granby** machine shops at Grand Forks where all repairs for the mines and smelters were done.

The original plan for the **Granby** Phoenix mines involved underground working. But open-pit mining also went on in the early days, and in some years fully 50 per cent of production came from this method. By 1905 **Granby** was the backbone of the Boundary. It employed more men — and it mined, shipped and smelted more ore — than all of the district's other companies combined. It was the springboard for all other copper successes in the Boundary.

Less successful was the million-dollar British Columbia Copper Co., founded in 1898 by a New York group to acquire the **Mother Lode** claim in Deadwood Camp. The proprietors thought there was sufficient ore in sight to justify the building of a smelter. Erected at Greenwood in 1899-1900 by Paul Johnson, it became active in February 1901. The smelter boasted the highest smokestack in B.C. — 120 feet high, 12 feet in diameter, and containing 220,000 bricks.

One of the two steam shovels owned by Granby at the Phoenix mines.

Granby's open pit copper mine at Phoenix, with steam shovel and electrified ore removal tramway.

GRANBY MINING COMPANY

GRANBY MINING COMPANY

Mine blasting in the early years was handled on or near the surface. When a whistle blew the warning, people from the nearby houses would rush out to the reinforced shelters provided by the company. (Only one fatal accident was reported — a woman failed to hear the warning and was killed by a rock crashing through her house.) In 1912 the company set off the biggest bang ever heard in the Boundary country. The blast took two years to prepare, with about 5000 holes drilled for 50,000 pounds of dynamite. The windows were boarded up in the surrounding houses and the inhabitants were told to take a day's holiday. Detonation shook the countryside and allegedly so diluted the ore that it could no longer be profitably smelted. The smelter struggled on for another six years but closed forever when the copper market collapsed in 1918. The community of **Mother Lode** was abandoned.

A third smelter was located at Boundary Falls, some three miles from Greenwood. Its chequered career was prompted by a need to

A close-up of Granby's steam shovel at the Phoenix mines.

GRANBY MINING COMPANY

165

service the Brooklyn claims at Phoenix owned by the Dominion Copper Co., in which railway contractors Mackenzie & Mann had a large interest. Back in 1900-01 they had employed James Breen, the smelter expert who built Trail and Northport smelters, to appraise the situation. He handed in a negative report and the mine closed down. Meanwhile, the Montreal & Boston Copper Co. had been building a small two-furnaced steam-operated smelter at Boundary Falls, and in the summer of 1904 it arranged with Dominion Copper to re-open the **Brooklyn** mine and smelt the ore at Boundary Falls. Eight months later Montreal & Boston went broke and Samuel Newhouse, a wealthy mining operator from Salt Lake City, with extensive properties in Utah and Colorado, took over. The new owner could not make it go and in 1908 it came into the hands of British Columbia Copper. It closed, never to re-open, in November, 1918.

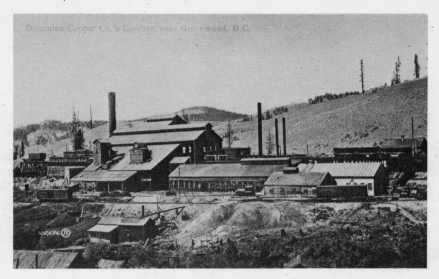

Dominion Copper Company's smelter at Greenwood, B.C.

Rawhide, Gold-Drop and Snowshoe mines, Phoenix, 1909.

The only mine in the Boundary country to be developed by English capital, and the only major one not tied up to a Boundary smelter, was the **Snowshoe**. Development was promoted by the backers of the British Columbia (Rossland & Slocan) Syndicate Ltd., a London-based diversified company owning mines and mineral claims in the Kootenays, real estate in Rossland and Nelson, and shares in a local mining journal. Shareholders of "the Snowshoe Gold Copper Mines" included some of the most prominent merchants of the City of London. The chairman was the Earl of Chesterfield; his deputy, George S. Waterlow — son of Sir Sidney Waterlow, a Lord Mayor of London — acted as executive director. From 1899 to 1901 the company pumped $130,000 into development. It took out some 100,000 tons of ore but found difficulties in getting it smelted. Finally the mine was leased to the Consolidated Mining & Smelting Co., who produced 500,000 tons more for their smelter at Trail.

Employment in the Boundary smelters at their peak ran into thousands. They helped to create towns like Grand Forks, Phoenix and Greenwood, where ten years before the region had been a wilderness. The smelters were one of the main markets for Crow's Nest coal, providing many jobs in the coal mines of the Kootenays and treating huge tonnages of copper ore. At one time Boundary copper was produced at the lowest price in the world. Operating costs for the Granby organization came down from $4.77 per ton in 1901 to $2.39 in 1913. Many factors contributed to this result, including economies of operating on a large scale, even though the grade was lower than any that had been worked before. In the twenty years from 1897 to 1917, copper production in B.C. rose from a mere $250,000 to $114,000,000.

But by the end of the war in 1918, the world's demand for copper had evaporated. The victorious allies had stockpiled a two-year supply. Copper prices dropped and the mines began to close. The year 1919 was the most unsatisfactory that the copper industry had experienced; obviously the decrease in home consumption and absence of foreign orders called for drastic action.

A permanent shutdown was announced at the **Granby** mines in Phoenix in the middle of 1919. Departures from Phoenix became a daily occurrence. All the hotels were boarded up. C.P.R. service dwindled to two mixed trains per week. The Great Northern began to dismantle its tracks. The banks closed down their branches. Houses were available for five dollars. Prime real-estate properties of ten years ago reverted to the government because nobody wanted to pay taxes on them, and by 1920 Phoenix was a ghost town.

A similar blight hit all the other Boundary towns. The smelters at Boundary Falls and Greenwood closed early. Machinery from Grand Forks and the compressor station at Knob Hill were shipped to the new Granby operation at Anyox, and skilled smelter personnel moved to that northern town. The copper industry in the Boundary country shut down for a long sleep. Not until Granby came back to Phoenix in 1956 with open-pit mining did the Boundary experience any new mining activity.

The scene now shifts to the coastal regions — to the little community of Britannia, 35 miles north of Vancouver on what is now the scenic motor road up Howe Sound to the ski resorts of Garibaldi. In the prosperous days of the **Britannia** copper mine there was no road, no railway, only the daily call of the Union steamship. Vancouver was a day's journey away.

Prospecting had been going on in the islands and mainland north and west of Burrard Inlet since the country had been opened up to miners in the gold-rush days. Dr. A.A. Forbes, medical officer to the Indians of the coast region, was the first to interest himself in the copper ore on Britannia Mountain. It is said that in 1893 he went to

In recognition of those who, from copper mine and smelter, served in World War I. Phoenix War Memorial, 1914-18.

Re-activating Phoenix in 1956. Repairing workers' houses.

GRANBY MINING COMPANY

see the Minister of Mines in Victoria to seek assistance in developing some of his claims. When this was refused, the good doctor's interest in the property vanished. Oliver Furry, a trapper living on the west side of Howe Sound, then took up the task. He drew in Joseph Boscowitz, a Victoria businessman, who enlisted Howard S. Walters from Montana and organized the Britannia Copper Syndicate Ltd. to develop the property. A little work was done but more funds were needed. The Syndicate was re-organized, bringing in Edgar Dewdney, a pioneer of the province and at one time its Lieutenant-Governor. The banking firm of Moore & Sichley of New York agreed to raise the money in its local market. By this time (1904) some 150 acres had been cleared and a store and several homes were built at the Beach. Meanwhile, a holding company had been created, for some reason under the laws of the State of Maine: the Howe Sound Co.

The ore went into the furnaces of a Vancouver Island smelter at Crofton which Britannia had bought. This smelter had been built by Henry Croft, brother-in-law of coal baron James Dunsmuir, under contract with the Lenora Mining Co. to treat the ore from its mine on Mount Sicker.

The mine and townsite at Britannia and the smelter at Crofton all came under the Howe Sound Co., which also owned copper mines in Mexico. The boom years for copper before World War I put the mine on a firm foundation. The latest equipment had been installed: a mile-long aerial tramway; five miles of industrial railway with gasoline as the motive power (an innovation in those days); a 200-ton concentrator. The ore reserves would last for many years. Then came August 4, 1914. Metal markets disintegrated immediately and a wire came from the New York office: "Close the mine." Local management tended to turn a blind eye to head-office requests but production was cut by 50 per cent.

Like all mining enterprises, Britannia had its share of natural disasters. In the early hours of March 22, 1915, the mountainside fell on the camp at the 1050-foot level. Newsmen from Vancouver arriving that afternood found, in the words of Bruce McKelvie of the *Province*:

> The mine office, store, rock crusher, tram terminus, a big bunkhouse, and half a dozen homes had been blotted out by millions tons of rock, mud and snow, which in some places were piled 50 feet deep over what had been the level of the camp.

It was comparable in horror and tragedy to the slide at Frank, Alberta, in 1903. Between 50 and 60 people died and 22 more were injured. It cost the company $210,000 in property damage alone.

In damage to property and lives there is not much difference between a landslide and a flood — or so the people of Britannia Beach found out in October 1921. It had been raining in torrents for several days and a natural driftwood dam holding the water in the creek high above the town gave way about 9 p.m. on a Sunday night. A five-foot wall of water rushed through the residential section, taking many houses with it into Howe Sound. "The place," said an eyewitness, "looks like a prairie town which has been struck by a cyclone."

Only in 1924, after the double blow of the general slump of 1919 and the 1921 flood, did continuous operation resume at the mine. The peak came in 1928 with a record production of 1,661,225 tons. Then came the Depression; the price of copper dropped to an all-time low of 5 and 7/8ths cents per lb. Salaries and wages were cut and the staff put on a part-time basis. Further staff cuts were made from a high of 1100 men in 1928 to 548 in 1932.

As Hitler's war approached, the B.C. mining picture began to improve. Instead of operating on 10 per cent of capacity, the mine worked up to 20 per cent, then to 30 and 50 and on to its normal tonnage.

B.C. MINISTRY OF MINES

Concentrator of the Britannia copper mine at Britannia Beach, Howe Sound, 1922.

In the lean years after 1945, when the head office in New York would not even authorize the purchase of a can of paint to redecorate company houses, the mine carried on. The Korean war and the upsurge in demand for metals gave Britannia a short break, but the ore was becoming exhausted. The Howe Sound Company pulled out and in January 1963, Anaconda Copper stepped in to the tune of (it is said) $4 million. A little earlier, the isolation of the community had been broken by the building of both railway and highway. Today it is just an hour's drive from downtown Vancouver. In 1974 the mine closed its tunnels and tramways for the last time.

Further up the coast was Anyox, a name that was synonymous with copper for 20 years. It is located on Granby Bay 110 miles from Prince Rupert, on the west shore of Observatory Inlet and 35 miles from its mouth. A range of steep timber-clad mountains separates

169

Observatory Inlet from Portland Canal. Four glacial creeks flow into Granby Bay, the most important from a mining standpoint being Hidden Creek. The area is rich in copper-bearing ores.

All the commercial ore bodies seem to have been known to the Indians long before the turn of the century when fishermen and cannery operators began to come into the area. In 1898 three Indian chiefs approached Archdeacon William Henry Collinson, an Anglican missionary, and told him of a mountain of gold at the head of Hastings Arm. He set out with some companions in a rowboat to investigate. On the way back, empty-handed, his party camped at the mouth of Bonanza Creek, one of the creeks which flows into Granby Bay, and the reddish color of the rocks prompted him to stake the area. It became the site of the **Bonanza** copper mine, bought by Granby in 1912. In the summer of 1899 his son Max with two prospectors went up Hidden Creek and staked what was to be Granby's **Hidden Creek** Mine.

WESTERN MINER

Brought into production by Granby Consolidated Mining & Smelting Company prior to World War I, the Hidden Creek mine at Anyox, B.C.

M.K. Rodgers, representing Marcus Daly (the great copper tycoon of Butte, Montana), then came into the district looking for promising properties. He obtained options on several claims in the Hidden Creek area, but for the next few years it was an on-and-off proposition. A little development work was done before the Daly estate pulled out. Then J.H. Hilles, another mining promoter, put in two years of development work — stopped in its tracks by the financial panic of 1907. M.K. Rodgers, having left the Daly interests, purchased the Hidden Creek claims on his own and put in $250,000 for development work. This turned out to be a bigger project than his Montana backer could handle and Granby Consolidated took it over in 1910.

The Phoenix mining office of Granby Consolidated had been looking at many properties, including Copper Mountain near Princeton, but all of them had proved disappointing. Finally O.B.

Smith, mining superintendent at Phoenix, submitted a list of potential properties to the directors in New York. They were asked to choose between Hidden Creek in northern B.C., Chelan in Washington and Flin Flon in Manitoba. They chose Hidden Creek, thereby keeping the business of the company within British Columbia.

Building began in 1912. At the mine, a mile and a half up Hidden Creek, the new camp included 50 cottages with electric light, hot and cold running water (the ultimate convenience in those days) and a dish-washing machine. According to the annual report of the B.C. Minister of Mines for 1912, "The confidence of this company in the mineral resources of the surrounding country is shown by its extensive investments."

These investments included a $3,600,000 construction program. The smelter had as its vital unit three water-jacketed rectangular copper-smelting furnaces. A dam was built one mile back of the smelter site for the generation of hydro power. All buildings were of permanent construction; the town itself had a hospital, a hotel, a recreation hall and 100 cottages. There were mess facilities and sleeping quarters for 600 men. The streets were laid out systematically with planked walks and roadways lighted by electric arc-lights. As the Minister of Mines reported, "The year 1913 has been a most notable one, Anyox having in a very short time sprung from a small mining camp into a smelter city."

A great smelter town on the coast. The waterfront at Anyox, with the Grand Trunk Pacific Railway coastal steamer from Vancouver.

It was no small achievement to plan, build and equip a modern industrial town within a space of two years and 550 miles from the sources of major supplies. Anyox was one of several industrial towns established by private companies in B.C. in the first decade of this century. Powell River, Ocean Falls and Swanson Bay come to mind, but these were all pulp-and-paper towns. Anyox was the first industrial town connected with the mining industry in the province (other than Ladysmith) that was systematically planned, laid out, and built before any metal was produced.

Tyee smelter, Ladysmith, 1902.

Logistics always presented problems. Granby was probably the first mining company in B.C. to go into long-haul coast barging. Under Captain James Griffiths of Seattle, a pioneer shipping man of the Pacific Northwest, it gave most of the business to the Coastwise Steamship & Barge Co. Large amounts of freight and heavy machinery were barged from Seattle or Vancouver up the inside passage, a new venture in coast transportation.

All urban needs of this isolated town were met by the company. Meals could be had at the company mess for $1 per day, and room in the company boarding-house went for $5 per month. A worker's family could be housed in a company-owned house for $17,50 monthly. By an arrangement with the Workmen's Compensation Board, all men employed by the company in Anyox paid a monthly hospital fee of $1. This entitled them to medical treatment and hospital and surgical care in all conditions arising from accident. The company built, staffed and ran its own hospital. In the words of P.A. O'Farrell of the *Province*:

> At Anyox I found (October, 1917) a complete city and seaport, an excellent hotel and three churches. I also went through the wards of one of the best equipped hospitals in Canada.

The ores of Hidden Creek were not self-fluxing like those in the Boundary country; for economical treatment, they had to be mixed with ores from other sources — the mines developed in Observatory Inlet and even some in adjacent Alaska.

> The company has carried out a vigorous campaign to acquire new properties in many districts, particularly in Alaska where three new mines have been acquired. . . . The ore from these mines will all be brought to the company smelter at Anyox for treatment. (B.C. Minister of Mines Report 1914)

The nature of the ground at Hidden Creek mine, Anyox, about 1912.

By 1915, after a couple of anxious years at Anyox, Granby occupied a dominant position in mining in B.C. The company's many sites mined and smelted 62.5 per cent of the province's ore production and produced 66.7 per cent of its copper.

Constant efforts were made to improve operations. Originally coke had been made at Union Bay on Vancouver Island and shipped up coast by barge. In 1918 Granby started its own coke plant at Anyox from coal shipped out of its own mine at Cassidy near Nanaimo. Investigations had started as early as 1915 into the flotation process of copper separation. These resulted in a new concentrator at Anyox, built in 1924 and reaching a production peak of 5,600 tons per day in 1935.

Through the Depression years the company kept the smelter going to sustain employment. Early in 1935 it had an unsold stock on hand of three years of production, and the decision was made to liquidate the company's holdings and close down Anyox. All northern properties went to the Consolidated Mining & Smelting Co. of Trail. People began to move out by the hundreds; a few had jobs and places to go to, but most of them had no money and no prospects. They crowded onto the **Prince Rupert** or **Prince George** and came to swell the ranks of the unemployed in Vancouver or Victoria. Many even abandoned their furniture — left in the house or at the Anyox dock.

The plant was dismantled by the A.R. Williams Machinery Co. of Vancouver, whose barges went southward with thousands of tons of scrap and machinery. A crew of 100 men took more than a year to finish the dismantling. The site has now reverted to the wilderness. The dense underbrush yields no trace of what was once the busiest smelter town in B.C.

West of Princeton, new opportunities had arisen on Copper Mountain. It was discovered in 1884 and staked in 1892; development work started in 1905 by a group associated with B.C. Copper. By 1920 a concentrator at Allenby and a railway from

B.C. MINISTRY OF MINES

An interior operation— the concentrator of the Allenby Copper Company at Allenby, on Copper Mountain near Princeton, 1923.

Princeton had been built. But in the copper slump after the armistice of 1918 the operation had to close. It was bought by Granby in 1923 and ran from 1925 to the start of the Depression, when again it had to close down. In November 1936 the directors of the company authorized the re-opening of the mine. Townsites were built at Allenby and Copper Mountain and a power plant

173

burning local coal was constructed at Princeton. It operated successfully for the next twenty years and closed for good in 1957 when the reserves became exhausted.

In the fifties Granby began a reappraisal of the old mines at Phoenix. It was found that parts of the original ore body still remained mainly on the roofs and floors of the old workings, and might be profitably recovered by open-pit methods. The property was repurchased from private sources and open-pit mining with power shovels and trucks started in 1956. The mine is still being worked (1976) but an end is definitely in sight.

The re-emergence of a strong postwar Japanese economy created a demand for raw materials. Japanese industrialists began to look overseas, especially at mineral deposits in British Columbia. The sixties set an all-time high for prospecting, exploration and new mining development in B.C. More than 75 major mining companies, as well as several hundred smaller ones, sought to uncover the hidden wealth locked in the mountains of this province. At least 2,000 professionals — prospectors, engineers, geologists and other exploration people — were active in the search for new mineral deposits. From a low of $5 million in 1960, by the middle of the decade more than $20 million per year was spent in prospecting and exploration.

Truck dumping its load into the primary crusher, at the Gibraltar copper mine near Williams Lake.

GIBRALTAR MINES LTD.

A 100-ton ore truck engaged in hauling ore from Gibraltar's open pit mine to the mill.

Mining methods began to change. The evolution of heavier earthmoving equipment — 200-ton trucks, and shovels with a capacity of 15 cubic yards or more — has made possible the huge open-pit mine. Millions of tons of overburden could thus be removed at an economical cost and the ore bodies exposed and worked as far down as 1000 feet. Production could be maintained seven days a week at fantastic rates — 40,000 or 45,000 tons per day. The problem of finding enough money to bring a mine into production, so difficult in earlier days, was eased by the eagerness of big Japanese companies to advance capital and by the willingness of Canadian and U.S. banks to loan money to big international mining corporations.

Many copper properties known to an earlier generation of prospectors now began to receive attention. One of the areas of early interest in the sixties was the Highland Valley, lying about 20 miles southeast of Ashcroft. From where the Bethlehem copper mine is now located a small tonnage of high-grade ore had been shipped as far back as 1915-16. Several other companies had worked the property as well, with little result. This was the state of things until the summer of 1954 when the Heustis-Reynolds-McLallan Syndicate re-staked some 100 claims. In February 1955 the mineral rights were transferred to a newly created entity: the Bethlehem Copper Corporation. This led to a new boom and the next 15 years saw the opening of ten new major copper mines in the province.

An exploration program at Bethlehem turned up an area of wide mineralization. The attention of the American Smelting & Refining Co. was attracted, to the tune of $1,250,000 in exploratory work. For various reasons the option was dropped; Bethlehem re-possessed and pushed ahead with development. Results persuaded the Sumitomo group of companies of Japan to provide enough funding to put the property into production, and to agree to purchase all concentrates for ten years. The development of the mine and the construction of the concentrator and service

GIBRALTAR MINES LTD.

Interior of concentrator at Gibraltar's copper mine, with rod and ball mills in background, and flotation cells in foreground.

buildings were completed by November 1962, with Northern Construction and J.W. Stewart as the prime contractor. This was the first major copper development in the Highland Valley and one of the first in the copper boom of the sixties.

Highland Valley became a magical name in the annals of mining in B.C. From the time of Bethlehem Copper's original surveys there has been continuous exploration in the valley which led to another great mine — **Lornex** — and several smaller ones like **Alwin**. Still awaiting development in 1976 are the 424 claims of Valley Copper, a Cominco venture and reportedly a rich property.

175

All the benefits of urban living. The post office at Logan Lake, serving Lornex copper mine.

CANADA POST

Since the coming of the Japanese mining men in the mid-fifties, many copper mines have been opened in various parts of the province. Out of the 15 copper-producing mines in 1974, ten are in the major league.

There will be new copper mines in B.C. in the years ahead, despite the impact of environmentalists and the inflated costs of labor, supplies and services. The people of the world will continue to demand articles containing copper, articles that have contributed so much to their standard of living. But the successful launching of new mines involves a great deal more than the discovery of new ore bodies. Tremendous new amounts of capital will be needed. The new techniques of open-pit mining require millions of tons of waste to be lifted before a pound of copper can be recovered. If a find is located in a remote and sparsely inhabited region, much money and effort will have to be expended to develop a management team and to offer the workers an attractive standard of living.

After six years. The township of Granisle in 1976.

GRANBY MINING COMPANY

The ferry between Granisle copper mine and the townsite, with the pathway cleared through the ice by artificial means.

Drilling at Granisle copper mine on Babine Lake. February 24, 1969.

As in the past, so in the future — British Columbia will have to look to Japan for expansion in its copper mines. The province now supplies about 32 per cent of the Japanese copper requirements, and tomorrow's needs may be even greater. In 1975, there were 19 copper exploration and development projects in B.C. which could be brought into production. Under favorable conditions some or all of these projects could blossom into new mines with a further strengthening of the provincial economy.

Re-activated Phoenix mine, 1956.

GRANBY MINING COMPANY

Prospecting, 1914— Giscombe portage, north central British Columbia.

How supplies came to prospecting and mine-developing parties in the field prior to World War I: A pack train leaving Hazelton.

10

Minerals in the Minor League

The mainstays of the B.C. mining industry have been gold, coal and copper, in that order. These minerals have enjoyed a world-wide demand for two hundred years or more and have absorbed most of the attention — in money and manpower — of the mining industry in this province. But other minerals have contributed to industrial growth here as well. Silver, lead and zinc all played a great part in the mineral development of the East and West Kootenays. Under the right market conditions lesser-known minerals such as mercury and tungsten made their contributions, and in more recent years even rarer metals (such as cadmium, bismuth and indium) have been refined to a state of high purity and found ready markets, especially in the electronics industry.

Other than gold, coal and copper, the mineral to grab the most headlines has been iron ore. It was iron ore that put the island of Texada on the front page of every newspaper in the province a hundred years ago. Harry Trim was a timber cruiser employed by Moody, Dietz and Nelson, the proprietors of the Moodyville sawmill in what is now North Vancouver. In the early 1870s, while cruising to find suitable timber stands he discovered an outcrop of iron ore on the northern end of Texada Island three miles from Gillis Bay. He broke off a sample and showed it to Sewell Prescott Moody back in Moodyville. At that point Moody became very excited and arranged for the company ship (the *Cariboo Fly*) to take himself and several employees of the sawmill to Texada to pre-empt large sections of land covering the deposits. Fourteen pre-emptions by employees of Moody, Dietz & Nelson were filed at New Westminster. Furthermore, Moody opened an ore mine account in the books of the sawmilling firm and drew many of the extraordinary expenses from it. As part of his plans to form a company to promote the discovery, he made a trip to Victoria and offered shares to Premier Amor de Cosmos and other members of the government. Shortly afterwards the premier left for a trip to

The famous iron mine on Texada Island, which led to the overthrow of Amor de Cosmos' provincial government. Pictured here when it belonged to the Puget Sound Iron Company, in 1901.

B.C. MINISTRY OF MINES

B.C. GOVERNMENT

Texada iron mine, with stockpile of ore loading wharf and ore carrier. Millions of tons of iron ore has been shipped from here to Japan.

England — ostensibly on government business, but in the eyes of most British Columbians to try and sell the Texada iron ore mine to moneyed men in London.

In an unsuccessful effort to unseat the government, the opposition member from Nanaimo rose in the provincial legislature and charged "that prominent members of the late and present government were in a ring to acquire possession of Texada Island in a manner prejudicial to the interests of the public." A Royal Commission was set to investigate the charges under Chief Justice Matthew Begbie. He and his fellow commissioners found:

> Although there were suspicious circumstances surrounding the pre-emptions on Texada Island in August, 1873, there was not sufficient evidence to believe that prominent or any members of the late or present governments were in a ring to acquire possession of Texada Island in a manner prejudicial to the interests of the public.

Nevertheless, a company was formed by Hugh Nelson, Sewell Moody and Robert P. Rithet (a prominent Victoria importer and exporter), with Amor de Cosmos, M.P.P. (recently resigned as premier) as sales representative. The object was to try and sell the property to eastern Canadian interests. Certainly the property had some potential value. The demand for rails in the proposed Canadian Pacific Railway's Pacific division was estimated at 9000 tons per annum. An ideal site for the erection of an iron works was owned by the Union Coal Mining Co. in the Comox district along with 1000 acres of rich undeveloped coal land. (This was to be developed by Dunsmuir a few years later into his valuable Cumberland coal mines.) It was only 18 miles away from Texada by water, which could provide the cheapest form of transportation for the iron ore. The promoters' large ideas envisioned a coal-iron-steel complex similar to the one created a few years later by U.S. capital at Sydney on Canada's east coast. Their concept was to supply the whole Pacific northwest with iron and steel for the railways and foundries and the hardware trade. The reality, though, has continued to elude regional businessmen both north and south of the border. These efforts did mark the first practical steps towards an iron and steel industry in B.C.

The east was not interested but apparently the south was. The publicity surrounding the Texada iron ore deposits came to the ears of certain California businessmen who were planning a small blast furnace and pig-iron manufactory near Port Townsend in Washington Territory. Their company, the Puget Sound Iron Co., acquired the Texada iron deposits and in the late 1870s began to work it and ship the ore to the ironworks at Irondale. For the next 36 years the Texada iron mine was engaged (sometimes intermittently, as in 1904 when the furnace at Irondale closed down) in supplying the Washington plant. Texada iron went into the construction of several of the American warships built on the west coast in this period. The most famous was the U.S.S. *Oregon*, which made the spectacular rush from the west to the east coast around the Horn to support her sister ships in their blockade of Cuban ports during the Spanish-American war.

In this period, there was much international interest in B.C. iron ores. On Cherry Bluff near Cherry Creek station, on the C.P.R. main line 12 miles west of Kamloops, Dr. G.M. Dawson of the Geological Survey of Canada had noted a deposit of iron ore as far back as 1877. The claim was staked by J.W. MacKay in 1888 and the Glen Iron Mining Co. was formed. It shipped 750 tons in the summer of 1890 to the Tacoma smelter and 200 tons to the new smelter just erected at Revelstoke. In 1893 the blast furnace at Irondale took 500 tons; more would have been shipped but for the business depression which struck that year. In the next two years, 2000 more tons went to the smelter at Tacoma. D. Gilman of Seattle, president of the Lake Shore & Eastern Railway, became interested in the mine as a potential source of supply to an ironworks and manufacturing plant proposed in the Seattle neighborhood for the manufacture of railway cars. But the financial panic of 1893, followed by an extensive business stagnation, killed the proposal. The mine worked intermittently until 1913 providing flux to the Nelson and Trail smelters. It was operated as an open-pit mine, and by the time it closed there was a hole in the bluff 150 feet deep.

The whole question of bringing iron ore deposits into production in B.C. has always hinged on the demand. With limited manufacturing facilities in the Pacific northwest, as well as an abundance of industrial minerals and lumber for building purposes, it was almost impossible to interest capitalists in the building of iron and steel works. Steel of all shapes and sizes could be and was more cheaply imported from the eastern U.S. than it could ever be made in B.C. or Washington State. Therefore iron ore deposits attracted very little attention from entrepreneurs or investors until the Japanese economy boomed in the fifties.

It had long been known that a huge tonnage of iron ore lay locked up in the deposits that had so intrigued Amor de Cosmos and his

Deep-sea loading facilities and stock pile of the Zeballos Iron Mines Ltd., at Zeballos on the west coast of Vancouver Island. This mine was only in operation four years; all of its ore was shipped to Japan.

colleagues in the seventies. The Geological Survey of Canada conservatively estimated in 1916 that these deposits held more than 4,500,000 tons. Thus, when the Japanese began to scout the world for iron ore to supply their steel plants, Texada Island did not escape their notice. Supported by the Japanese, a U.S. company was formed in May 1951 (the Texada Mines Ltd), to explore this property by diamond drilling. By the end of the year roads had been built and deep-sea docking facilities prepared. In 1952 all the installations were built: a concentrator, power plant, staff accommodation, and the like. The open-pit operation within a year had started to ship an annual volume of 350,000 tons of concentrates to Japan. Open-pit mining continued for another 12 years and then operations went underground. For another ten years, hundreds of thousands of tons went annually from underground operations to Japan. Before closing in 1975, it was a major economic factor on the island and had provided jobs for hundreds of British Columbians.

To meet growing Japanese demands, Jedway Iron Ore Ltd. (a subsidiary of Granby Mining Co.) in 1961 signed a contract with Sumitomo Shoji Kaisha Ltd. of Tokyo; Jedway undertook to supply 2 million tons of iron ore concentrate over five years, to be taken from claims not then developed at Harriet Harbour on the southeastern coast of Moresby Island in the Queen Charlottes. It took four years to bring the open-pit mine into production with the building of a deep-sea wharf and the necessary separating and concentrating plant. Mining ceased on February 28, 1968, the contract having been completed; the last shipment of concentrate was delivered a couple of months later. In all, more than 2 million tons of concentrate had been shipped to Japan during the seven years of operation.

Also on Moresby Island, on its west coast on Tasu Sound, is the Wesfrob iron mine of Falconbridge Nickel Mines Ltd., producing since 1967. This is a $40 million investment to supply a million tons of iron and copper concentrates to Japan over ten years. The decision to begin construction of the mining plant was made in 1964. Everything had to be done from scratch: logging off the open-pit area and the townsite; leveling off the plantsite; pushing the access roads to mine, plant and townsite; building a power plant, concentrator and other mining installations, as well as accommodation and school and recreational facilities for the workers; and providing a deep-sea terminal to service the giant ore carriers of 50,000 tons or more. As of 1977, this was the last producing iron-ore mine in B.C., and was expected to go underground in 1978. Millions of tons of ore remain to be mined, but as the price of iron ore has been relatively stable for the last ten years and the price of wages and supplies has risen with inflation, the profit outlook is grim. There is considerable doubt over future operations.

The non-metallic branch of the B.C. mining industry can be traced back for more than 100 years. Building stones have been quarried near the coastal cities since the 1870s, even though lumber is so plentiful that the use of stone for building is too expensive for all but the most unusual cases. Stone was much used in the past, though, for public buildings of note and for big hotels and office blocks. The United States Mint in San Francisco, constructed in 1870, was built of stone from Newcastle Island near Nanaimo. In more recent years Newcastle stone has been used in B.C.'s pulp and paper plants as pulping stones. Haddington Island on the northeastern coast of Vancouver Island, situated on Broughton Strait four miles east of Alert Bay, is famous for the high quality of its building stones. The exterior of the legislative buildings in Victoria is built of this stone, chosen by the architect (Francis Mawson Rattenbury) for its light color and superior qualities of moulding and dressing. Work at the quarry was very erratic: when contracts came up for important public buildings in Victoria or Vancouver it was re-opened and when there was no demand it remained closed. The last time in action was the late twenties when it provided stone for the new Hotel Vancouver and the Royal Bank buildings in Vancouver.

Taylor's quarry on Saturna Island supplied the sandstone in 1904 for the Carnegie Public Library (now the Greater Victoria Public Library). Gabriola Island stone provided the exterior of the old Victoria post office building that went up in 1896 facing the Inner Harbour. In Vancouver, the Flack Block at Cambie and Hastings is built of Gabriola Island stone. But today all the quarries are permanently closed; concrete, steel, aluminium and wood are much cheaper and find more favor with modern architects.

Granite is found on Nelson Island at the mouth of Jervis Inlet 60 miles north of Vancouver. All the granite used in the coastal cities of B.C. has come from this quarry. It was used for the piers of the Fraser River railway bridge at New Westminster in 1902; and in the steps leading up to the main entrance of the legislative buildings in Victoria.

A source of building stone for many buildings in British Columbia. Newcastle Island sandstone quarry, 1904.

Where millions of tons of limestone are quarried. The little settlement of Vananda on Texada Island.

Blubber Bay, Texada Island, 1916.

Where much of the early cement used in British Columbia was made. Vancouver Portland Cement Company's works at Tod Inlet near Victoria, on point of completion in 1904.

Limestone, one of the raw materials for cement and also for lime (a much-used commodity in the building trades), is found in great abundance around Blubber Bay on Texada Island. Here lie the largest limestone deposits in the Pacific northwest. In 1887 the first wood-fired lime kiln was built on the island. It worked only a short time and then closed down through lack of orders. J.J. Palmer built some kilns at Marble Bay in 1898, operated them for a short time and then sold out to the Tacoma Steel Co., which was anxious to obtain the limestone as a smelting flux. The real start of the limestone industry — the mainstay of the island — came in 1907 with the formation of the Pacific Lime Co. Now known as Domtar Chemicals Ltd. (Lime Division) a Canadian company with plants throughout the nation, it has supplied limestone and lime to the pulp and paper industry, steel mills, foundries and cement plants in B.C., Washington and Oregon for the last 70 years.

Tod Inlet, on the west side of Saanich peninsula some 18 miles from Victoria, used to be the home of the limestone quarry and cement works of the Vancouver Portland Cement Co. Here in 1904, Toronto capital erected the first cement plant in B.C. The operation was self-sufficient: limestone was mined a few yards back of the plant, electricity was produced in its own generators, and water transportation was provided by its own steamers loading at its own wharf. Here, until 1921, managing director R.P. Butchart ran a business whose product helped to build most of the big B.C. coastal construction projects of the time. At that date a new plant and quarry was opened up across the inlet at Bamberton which is still supplying the industry with cement. Through the imaginative planning of R.P. Butchart and his wife, the quarry at Tod Inlet was turned into the Butchart Gardens and is now a world-famous tourist attraction — as well as an outstanding example of a pioneer mining-reclamation scheme.

The cement industry on the lower mainland has kept pace with building requirements. In the mid-fifties a French multi-national company entered the B.C. business world by building a large cement manufacturing plant on Lulu Island. Canada Cement Lafarge Ltd., as it is now known, bought the Marble Bay quarries on Texada Island from the local Beale interests to ensure a source of limestone. This French company serving a Canadian market then turned to a famous British contractor to mechanize the operation. The B.C. division of John Laing & Co. got the contract. Today Canada Cement Lafarge Ltd. and Domtar Chemicals Ltd. quarry some 2 million tons each year from the limestone beds of Texada.

No story of mining in B.C. would be complete without tracing the phenomenal growth of Cominco. (The founding of the company has been dealt with in Chapter 8.) Today it exerts a powerful influence on the economy of the Kootenays and of the province. The company's major operations in B.C. are centered in two locations — Trail, the site of its non-ferrous smelting and refining complex and its large chemical fertilizer plants, and Kimberley, the site of the **Sullivan** mine with its large concentrator.

Trail, B.C., showing Cominco's operations.

Pouring slag at Trail smelter.

In the Sullivan concentrator, Kimberley, checking flotation.

British Columbia is a world leader in the production and refining of lead and zinc. The **Sullivan** mine is the largest single lead and zinc producer in the world. The basic problem faced by the management of Cominco in its early days was how to extract the base metals — lead, zinc and iron — from the **Sullivan** ores. It has been told in Chapter 8 how the exigencies of war caused an electrolytic zinc plant using **Sullivan** ore to be built at Trail in 1916. The process was too expensive for commercial use and had to be discontinued. But the search for better methods carried on, and in 1919 a differential flotation process was announced which made

185

possible the economic separation of Sullivan ore into high-grade concentrates of lead, zinc and iron. A flotation concentrator was built at Trail and operated successfully from 1920 to 1923. In 1923, a concentrator of 3000 tons daily capacity, built from the same design and for the same purpose, was constructed at Kimberley. This marked the turning-point in the affairs of the company. Supported by almost inexhaustible deposits of ore within the **Sullivan** mine which could be separated into the respective metals by a commercially proven process at a cost that the customers would pay, the company now had a firm basis for expansion.

The twenties saw a rapid growth in Cominco's metal production with large increases in the capacities of the lead and zinc refineries at Trail. Increases in the number of employees brought a boom to the Kootenay communities of Trail and Kimberley. This period also saw the separation of some of the rarer metals in the **Sullivan** ore — cadmium in 1927 and bismuth in 1928 — and their production in commercial quantities. These, along with indium (also found in the **Sullivan** ore and commercially produced in 1949), were the metals of the future. Bismuth, because of its resistance to high temperatures, became widely used in safety devices against fire and heat. Cadmium and indium became extensively used in the electronics industry in television sets and transistors.

COMINCO

Lead slabs ready to be shipped at Trail.

Cominco's mercury mine at Pinchi Lake, 1943.

B.C. MINISTRY OF MINES

The twenties also saw the beginnings of the first successful anti-pollution campaign in western Canada. Concerned citizens, including Washington State farmers and Canadian and U.S. government officials, added their voices to an international tribunal's in persuading the company to curtail the massive concentration of sulphur dioxide gas emitted from the smelter chimneys. The gases were thereupon contained and not allowed to escape into the air. From these gases the company began to make sulphuric acid, the forerunner of Cominco's vast fertilizer manufacturing plants. In 1931, the Trail fertilizer plant went into production, using the recovered sulphuric acid. This innovation launched the company into the agricultural market and into the making of industrial chemicals as the basis of its fertilizer products. The fields around Trail and south of the border once again became fertile and a major pollution problem had been solved.

Construction related to the fertilizer plant cushioned the first effects of the great Depression at Trail in 1930. A fall in the prices of lead and zinc and lack of demand forced the company to cut back on production. It had to lay off staff, cut wages, and clamp down on exploration and development. The Depression, though, enabled Cominco to acquire a controlling interest in Pacific Coast Terminals Ltd., the owners of the wharves at New Westminster where the greatest overseas tonnage of Trail's lead and zinc was embarked.

As the Depression weakened, the demands for re-armament (especially in Great Britain) boosted the price of metals again. War clouds gathered, and production was expanded to meet the needs of the allied nations. The "war minerals" — mercury and tungsten — came into great demand, mercury for detonators and tungsten to strengthen steel. Cominco developed and brought into production a mercury mine at Pinchi Lake and a tungsten mine near Hazelton. Special war factories, like the Canadian ordnance ammonium nitrate plant and the "heavy water" plant for the U.S., sprang up at Trail and disappeared as the needs vanished.

The end of the war and the reconstruction period saw a sustained demand for lead and zinc. In the early fifties serious consideration was given to that long-standing dream of many British Columbians, the establishment of a local iron and steel industry. New efforts began in the search for an economic basis for smelting the thousands of tons of iron ore contained in the tailings from the **Sullivan** mine. The work took ten years; in 1961, for the first time in the history of the province, pig-iron was produced from these tailings — the realization of a century-old dream.

A small blast furnace at Kimberley was the cradle of the first local iron industry fed on B.C. ore. It was only a small operation, providing 50,000 tons a year, but Cominco was looking ahead. It then acquired a local company in Vancouver (Western Canada Steel Ltd.) which had been producing steel by melting scrap. In 1966, an 80,000-ton plant for converting pig-iron into steel was built at Kimberley. A new rolling mill was built in Vancouver, representing the first fully integrated steel operation in western Canada whereby finished rolled-steel products were produced from B.C. ore. Unfortunately the economics of the situation made it impossible to continue the steel-making operation at Kimberley. Steel could be imported from Japan at a much lower cost, and the making of iron and steel in the Kootenays was discontinued in 1972. The facilities of Western Canada Steel in Vancouver are still used with profit to produce a wide range of steel products for British Columbian construction and manufacturing industries. But the dream of local steel mills supplied by B.C. ore has yet to be fully realized.

Power for the Trail smelter. Wanete Dam on Columbia River at the U.S. border.

Geologists underground in the H.B. mine.

Increasing power requirements of Trail and Kimberley demanded that the company's generating plants operate for many years at maximum capacity. The load was lightened by the building of the Wanete Dam and powerhouse, on the Pend-d'Oreille River where it joins the Columbia eleven miles south of Trail. This was the biggest power project the company had undertaken, with an initial cost of $35,000,000. Since 1955, when the first two units went into production, its capacity has been doubled. A transmission line connects Cominco's power grid with the Bonneville Power Administration's network south of the border and in times of shortage, power can be directed either way.

The basic unit in Cominco's increasingly complex organization is the mine. It has been the policy of the company since its inception to keep abreast of all mineral discoveries and if possible to option and investigate them. In the fifties, the company put three more B.C. mines into production. The famous **Bluebell** mine at Riondel (the oldest lead-zinc mine in B.C.) was reactivated and a concentrator was built and concentrates shipped to Trail. At Salmo in the Kootenays, the **H.B.** mine was brought into production in 1955, producing 1000 tons daily. In northwestern B.C. near the junction of the Tulsequah and Taku rivers, the third Cominco mine — **Tulsequah Chief** — started shipping lead and zinc concentrates to Trail in 1951.

Cominco, which originated in B.C. and has made so many outstanding contributions to the mineral development of the province, now operates throughout Canada and in many foreign countries. It has grown bigger than its B.C. base and is known around the world as a major mining company with many interests. Thus decisions made in other jurisdictions or spheres of company activity — such as that to develop the **Pine Point** mine in the Northwest Territories — could and often do have great

188

significance for B.C. mining. With the decision to ship **Pine Point** concentrates to Trail for smelting, an enlargement of the Trail smelter was imperative. On the other hand, the development of the **Vestgron** lead and zinc mine in Greenland has had no impact on the B.C. scene.

In the 1920's, the lead and zinc concentrates came down to Vancouver from the smelter at Trail, and were shipped on boats like the one above to customers overseas.

We now turn our attention to a mining venture unique in the annals of British Columbia. The **Cassiar** asbestos mine is the only one of its kind in the province, producing a mineral that has long been known and much sought after. Its heat-resistant properties make it invaluable for fireproofing and insulating materials, and in smaller quantities it goes into the making of 3000 other products. The mine is situated in the famous Cassiar placer-gold district of an earlier day. It is within 30 miles of the greatest of the placer creeks — named after its discoverer, McDame. But the riches now being uncovered in the district were beyond the dreams of the early gold-seekers. Those early pioneers noted the greenish rock on McDame mountain and listened to Indian tales of local birds building their nests with a fluffy material which would not burn in a forest fire. Over the years many a legend hung over McDame mountain but little notice was taken until the end of the Second World War when people began to come in from the Alaska Highway to prospect the country.

Victor Sittler had worked as a maintenance mechanic on the Alaska Highway when it was being built, and after the war he decided to come back to the north country to do some prospecting. With three partners, he set out on a prospecting trip in 1950 to the Cassiar country. On the western slope of McDame mountain at an altitude of 6,100 feet, they found a great outcropping of asbestos. They knew that they had found a good

189

thing but people did not seem to be interested. Then Fred M. Connell of Conwest Exploration Co. Ltd. sent up a geologist to look over the property — and the action began. Connell set up the Cassiar Asbestos Corporation Ltd., who drove in a series of exploration tunnels. This work proved that a large asbestos zone extended well below the peak of McDame mountain. To get to the ore it was decided to cut off the top of the mountain by the open-pit method. Over the years the entire top has been removed and to date more than 61,000,000 tons of rock and waste have been carted away. Even today it is calculated that nine tons of waste has to be removed for every ton of ore sent to the mill, an exceptionally high ratio. Commercial production started in 1953 and shows no sign of stopping. The townsite of Cassiar, built and run by the company, holds a population of 1500. The mine has been bringing as much as $40 million per year into the B.C. economy.

This chapter has outlined the story of the minerals of minor economic importance and the contributions that they have made to the development of the province. Lead and zinc have been, and still are, the most important. Their history is bound up with the growth of Cominco and the impact of these metals on the B.C. economy can best be measured in terms of the company as a whole.

Processing plant, Endako molyb-denum mine, Fraser Lake, British Columbia.

Scale model of the mill of Endako mine, Fraser Lake, taken about 1965.

Mining development in northern B.C. A company camp high in the mountains.

Planes began to be used after World War I to fly the
prospectors into remote areas, and to drop supplies
to geological survey parties. Here is an early Curtis
float plane at Alert Bay in 1920.

B.C. FOREST SERVICE

A Canadian Air Force plane used in mining and
forestry work. July 11, 1926.

B.C. FOREST SERVICE

A Consolidated Mining & Smelting Company's plane,
about 1935. On the Columbia River, just upstream
from Trail smelter. Tadanac residential area opposite.

COMINCO

Transportation to the mines in the 1960's. A Junkers
float plane.

B.C. FOREST SERVICE

A Prospectus for Prospectors

The mining industry in B.C. is emerging from the doldrums with a new interest in exploration and development. Changes in the provincial government's attitude towards the industry, coupled with a world-wide demand for energy resources, have spurred major mining companies into looking again at the mineral resources of this province — including the mineral potential of many geological byways.

Exploration and development have concentrated on coal, thanks to the province's large reserves and the need to develop energy resources other than oil. The B.C. government is encouraging private industry to play a larger part in contributing to Canadian and international expansion of the coal trade. In January, 1977, ten major development programs were under way: six in or near the Peace River coalfields and four in southeastern B.C.

Japan has recently provided the largest (and still growing) off-shore market for coal, but now concerted efforts are being made to sell in Mexico and Brazil. Nationally, the greatest interest is being expressed by Ontario, where Ontario Hydro has a contract to take 500,000 tons annually for fifteen years from Byron Creek Collieries at Corbin. Ontario steel-makers are involved in several B.C. development programs. Improved coal transportation technology is required to move coal at competitive prices to central Canada. Federal Industries Ltd., owners of Neptune Bulk Terminals in Vancouver, are now building a coal terminal at Thunder Bay to service western Canadian coal, to be completed late in 1978.

A sizable number of new coal mines can be expected in B.C. in the coming years. By 1980, some 10,000,000 tons per year could be moving to off-shore markets from the Peace River coalfields via Prince Rupert and Vancouver, with much more to follow.

Uranium, another energy mineral, has a three-year federal-provincial reconnaissance program. After deposits of this mineral were discovered southeast of Kelowna, many private firms began prospecting in the area. Claims recorded have raised dramatically in 1977 being 31% over those filed in 1976.

Copper is now the chief mineral extracted and exported from B.C., but the copper companies have undergone a difficult time. The world copper market is oversupplied, production has been kept high in the developing African and South American countries, inventories have been running at twice the normal size, and the price has often fallen below the cost of production. Further, an increasing share through royalties and taxation has been skimmed off by various governments. Molybdenum found so often in copper bearing ores is now experiencing a boom. Increasingly used in the steel industry it is helping turn some of B.C.'s major copper producers back into profitable operations.

British Columbia has many large low-grade deposits still undeveloped. Few of these could be profitably worked at present prices; one notable exception is Afton Mines near Kamloops, where a medium open-pit mine and smelter will come on stream late in 1977. The mine is working under a ten-year contract for 25,000 tons of refined copper annually with two British customers. World-wide consumption of copper is still increasing, though, and under the right conditions B.C. could still experience a copper boom to match that of the sixties.

Lead and zinc offer an encouraging outlook. Uses of lead are fast increasing, largely through demands for more electric storage batteries as a by-product of the energy crisis. Industrial research is now being directed to the improvement of lead-acid storage batteries, a potential field for vastly increased use of lead. For both lead and zinc, U.S. government policy on strategic stockpiling is increasing demand. It all means more work for Kimberley and Trail.

The long-term prospects for mining in B.C. are bright. The emphasis in exploration will be on the search for coal, uranium and high-grade copper deposits. World trade in metals is becoming increasingly competitive, which will force producers to use the most advanced cost-cutting techniques. A balance will have to be struck between concern for the environment and the need for economic growth. If new mining technologies can be introduced — and if the requirements of environmental control can be held within practicable limits and the governments seated in Victoria and Ottawa are responsive to the needs of the industry — then the people of B.C. can look with confidence to the future.

When the gasoline launch came in prior to World War I, prospecting, surveying and supply parties made use of the new invention on the lakes and rivers of B.C.

B.C. FOREST SERVICE

Transportation to the mines on Dease Lake trail, 1925.

B.C. MINISTRY OF MINES

B.C. FOREST SERVICE

The modern way of getting to the mines. A bombardier in the bush near Willow River, north central British Columbia.

195

Glossary

Abandonment: The act of relinquishing of work or of rights by absence or lapse of time or exhaustion of the mine.

Air-compressor: A machine for compressing air to a pressure sufficient to work machinery. Used in the early days mostly to work drills.

Anthracite coal: A hard black coal containing 85% to 95% carbon as against 70% to 85% for bituminous coal. A type of coal which produces a greater heat per unit than soft coal.

Area of mineralization: A region possessing mineral wealth of importance.

Asbestos: A name applied to a group of naturally fibrous minerals usually white or gray in color one of whose more important properties is that of being fire-resistant.

Assay: An examination of a mineral or ore to ascertain its properties and commercial value.

Assayer: One who examines minerals or ores to determine their values and properties.

Auriferous: A word denoting the presence of gold as in auriferous rock.

Bar: A bank of sand, gravel or other material which has accumulated along the bed or at the mouth of a river.

Beds of coal: Coal deposits.

Bedrock: Any solid rock overlain by layers of earth or gravel.

Beehive oven: An oven originally built in the form of an old-fashioned beehive. It had an opening at the top and various small ones at the base for draught. Used in the making of coke from coal.

Bismuth: A brittle silver-white metallic element. Widely used in safety devices against fire and heat.

Bituminous coal: Ordinary soft coal much used in electrical generation.

Blast: The explosion set off by explosive compounds to split rocks.

Blasting: The operation of splitting rocks by explosive charges.

Blasting powder: A powder containing materials (nitrate and sulphur, etc.) which can be detonated to produce an explosion.

Blast furnace: A furnace in which fuel is burned with an air blast to smelt ore in a continuous operation.

Blow-in: The act of starting up a blast furnace.

Blow-out: (In a coal mine) A sudden and violent escape of gas.

Bore: A tunnel at the time of its excavation.

Bullion: Uncoined gold or silver in the shape of bars, ingots or other convenient forms.

Cadmium: A white malleable ductile metal capable of a high polish. Much used in the electronic industry.

Check weighman: One who records the amounts of coal raised daily by coal miners.

Civil engineer: One whose work includes design, construction and maintenance of public works, highways, railroads, bridges, steel frames of buildings and the like.

Claim: The portion of land to which a prospector or miner is legally entitled on completion of the necessary documentation and work.

Coal: A solid, brittle, combustible rock much used in the generation of energy.

Coal bed or seam: A bed or stratum of coal.

Coal bunker: A place for storing coal.

Coal cutting machine: A machine worked by compressed air or electricity for undercutting or channeling a bed of coal.

Coal face: The working face of a stall or room composed of coal.

Coalfield: a region in which deposits of coal occur.

Coal mine: All parts of the property of a mining plant which contributes directly or indirectly under one management to the mining and handling of coal.

Coal washing: The operation by which coal is freed from its impurities by washing.

Coarse gold: Gold which is not rich. Gold which is inferior or faulty in character.

Coke: a soft coal after the gases have been expelled which when burnt gives off an exceptionally bright heat used in making steel, or in smelting other ores.

Coking coal: Coal especially suited for making coke.

Coke-oven: A chamber of brick or other fire resistant material in which coal is turned into coke.

Colliery: A coal mine.

Concentrates: The residue after separating the ore or other metal from its containing rock or earth. Concentrates then go to the smelter for further separation.

Concentrator: The plant including the machinery and buildings in which the concentrates are produced.

Compressor-station: The site in which a compressor or a battery of compressors are housed. These supply the air to run the drills and other mining machinery.

Copper: A common metal of reddish color ductile and malleable. One of the best conductors of heat and electricity.

Cribbing: A form of construction by piling logs or beams horizontally one above the other and spiking or chaining them together, each layer being at right angles to those above and below it.

Deep-diggings: Operations in a placer mining district carried on at a depth requiring shafts or tunnels.

Deep-pit mining: Mining carried on at a considerable depth below the surface.

Development tunnel: A tunnel bored for the purpose of testing an ore body.

Diamond drilling: The act or process of drilling holes using bits inserted with diamonds as the rock-cutting tool.

Differential flotation: A process separating complex ores into two or more valuable minerals by flotation.

Diggings: A district in which placer mining is carried on.

Dredge: A piece of machinery used for excavating underwater.

Dredging: The act of using a dredge.

Drill: A tool used for boring in hard material.

Drilling: To make a hole with a drill or similar tool.

Drift: A horizontal passage underground.

Drum: That part of the winding machinery at the top of the hoist on which the rope or chain is coiled.

Ductile: Capable of being permanently drawn or hammered thin.

Electrolysis: A process of chemical change resulting from the passage of an electric current. The process is of great value commercially in the refining of various metals.

Fault: (In coal mining) A portion of a seam of coal replaced by shale or sandstone.

Fineness of gold: The degree of purity of gold.

Flotation: A method of mineral separation in which froth created in water by a variety of agents floats some finely crushed minerals whereas other minerals sink.

Flume: A channel usually of wood for carrying water from a distance to be utilized for power transmission. Used extensively in placer mining.

Flux: A substance that absorbs the mineral impurities of a metal.

Free gold: Gold not combined with other substances.

Furnace charger: A weighing machine for feeding into the furnace mouth the proper proportions of ore, fuel and other materials.

Furnace crusting: A hard layer of mineral deposit within the furnace which for various reasons will not liquify.

Galena: A lead sulfide. The commonest ore of lead.

Geology: The science that deals with the structure of the earth especially as recorded in the rocks.

Geologist: One who is trained in the science of geology One who is an expert in the composition and structure of rocks.

Ghost town: A deserted mining community.

Gold: A heavy, soft, yellow, ductile, malleable metal. One of the heaviest substances known.

Gold bar or gold brick: Refined gold in the form of bricks or bars of convenient sizes and weights for handling and storage.

Gold bearing gravel: Gravel that holds a certain amount of gold.

Goldfield: A region where gold is found.

Gold fever: A mania for seeking gold.

Gold dust: Particles and flakes of gold obtained in placer mining.

Ground sluicing: A method of removing a thick surface layer of non pay-dirt from a layer of auriferous strata or bedrock by means of a stream of water. As the water flows the miners loose the dirt by pick and shovel. The stream carries away the gravel leaving the paydirt exposed for mining by ordinary sluicing.

Grubstake: Supplies furnished to a prospector in return for a promise of a share in his discoveries.

Hard-rock mining: That mining done in hard rock requiring much drilling and blasting.

High grade ore: Ore that contains a high portion of a valuable mineral.

Hoist: A device (usually power-driven) for raising ore or other material from a mine and lowering and raising men and supplies.

Hoisting cage: A frame with one or more platforms for men and cars used in hoisting in a vertical shaft.

Hydraulicking or Hydraulic mining: The method by which a head of water under great pressure is directed against a bank of gravel or a hillside which washes down the dirt into sluices where the gold is separated from the earth by gravity.

Hydraulic elevator: An apparatus used in dredging and hydraulic mining which raises mud and gravel by means of a jet of water under heavy pressure.

Indium: A soft malleable easily fusible silver-white metallic element that is resistant to tarnishing and resembles aluminum. Used in the aviation industry as plating for engine bearings.

Ingot: A mass of metal cast for convenient handling, storage or future working, but not in its final form.

Iron: The most abundant, most useful and most important of all metals found in the earth. It is malleable and ductile and can be worked into thousands of useful products by heating and cooling.

Leaching: Extracting a soluble metallic compound from an ore by dissolving it in a suitable solvent such as sulfuric acid.

Lead: A metallic element heavy, pliable and inelastic rarely occurring free from other substances in nature.

Lime kiln: A furnace for producing lime.

Lode: A deposit of valuable minerals between definite boundaries.

Lode-mine: A mine containing deposits or lodes of valuable minerals.

Low grade ore: Ore which only contains a small portion of valuable minerals.

Malleable: Capable of being extended, shaped or worked by hammering or rolling.

Mercury: A heavy silver-white metallic element that is a liquid at ordinary temperatures. Its principal source is cinnabar. Chief uses are in the manufacture of drugs and chemicals and in electrical control instruments.

Metals: A class of chemical elements found in nature generally characterized by ductility and malleability. Under the name of metals are found such well-known elements as iron, gold, silver, lead.

Metallurgy: The science and art of preparing metals from their ores by separating them from mechanical mixtures and chemical combinations.

Metallurgist: One who is trained in and practices the science and art of metallurgy.

Metallurgical processes: Processes involved in the extraction of metals from their ores.

Mine: An opening or excavation in the earth from which mineral matter of value is taken.

Miner: One who mines—one engaged in getting minerals out of the earth. Anyone working underground in a mine.

Mine rescue team: A group of trained mine rescue workers who go into a mine after an accident or explosion.

Minerals: Inorganic substances that can be extracted from the earth's crust for the use of man.

Mineralogy: The science connected with the study of minerals.

Mineralogist: One who is versed in the science of minerals. One who examines, analyzes and classifies minerals.

Mining camp: A settlement of miners, in the old days usually housed in very primitive conditions.

Mining claim: That portion of the public land which a miner takes and holds for mining purposes according to the mining laws of the country in which the land is situated.

Mining engineer: A man qualified by education, training and experience in the field of engineering as it relates to mining.

Molybdenum: A gray metal used in the making of high temperature alloys for use in missile and aircraft parts, reactor vessels, etc.

Non-ferrous: Metals not containing appreciable quantities of iron. Ores not worked primarily for their iron content.

Nugget: A small mass of metal such as gold or silver found free in nature.

Open-pit mining: A surface working open to the daylight A working in which the excavation is performed from the surface.

Ore: A mineral or a mineral-aggregate containing useful metals which can be mined with profit.

Outcrop or outcropping: When the ore comes out to the surface of the ground. Outcrops include those deposits that are so near the surface as to be found easily by digging.

Overburden: Used to designate material that is on top of a deposit of useful ore that can be mined from the surface by open-pit methods.

Packer: A person who transports goods by pack animals.

Pan (gold): A dish for washing sand and gravel or earth to obtain gold.

Panning: The simplest and most effective way of obtaining gold from river bars or sand banks. This is the process by which earth or gravel is washed in a gold-pan. By gravity gold drops to the bottom of the pan in the process of washing and is so recovered. A good placer miner may in a ten-hour day pan from one-half to one cubic yard, depending on the situation with regard to water and dirt.

Pay-dirt: any soil, sand or gravel containing gold in sufficient quantities to pay wages or better.

Per day by hand: In speaking of gold washed from a mine in the early days, the unit was the amount of gold obtained in one day by each man actually at work.

Pig-iron: Iron made by the reduction of iron ore in a blast furnace.

Pig-lead: Commercial lead in large oblong masses or pigs.

Pillar: An area of ore left in a mine intentionally for the purpose of ground control; that is, to support the roof or sides of a tunnel.

Pit-head: The top of a mine shaft usually including the buildings, roads, tracks, plant and machinery around it.

Placer: A place where gold is obtained by washing.

Placer gold: Gold obtained by means of running water or washing.

Placer mining: The extraction of gold from a placer deposit by running water.

Pocket of nuggets: A natural deposit of free gold in the form of nuggets.

Prospector: Somebody engaged in the exploration for valuable minerals.

Prospecting: The search with the objective of finding valuable minerals.

Precious metals: The uncommon and highly valuable metals such as gold and silver.

Pulping stones: Stones which are grooved by machine and used in the manufacture of mechanical wood pulp.

Quartz: Any hard rock or ore containing gold or silver as distinguished from sand and gravel.

Quartz mining: Mining for gold or silver in hard rock underground.

Reduction: The extraction of any metal from its ore. The term reduction is sometimes applied to the smelting process.

Reduction Works: The establishment in which the extraction of metal from its ores takes place. The term **reduction works** has sometimes been applied to designate a smelter.

Refinery: A term applied to a plant in which metal is extracted from its ore or concentrate.

Roasting: To heat to a point so as to expel from the ore impurities which would impede smelting.

Roasting ovens: Ovens especially built for roasting ores.

Rocker: A device constructed like a child's cradle by which placer miners in the early days obtained gold by means of water and agitation.

Rolling-mill: A manufacturing establishment in which metal is made into bars, rails or rods by working it between a pair of rollers.

Selective mining: A method of mining where the best ore is selected in order to make good mill returns leaving the low-grade ore in the mine.

Self-fluxing ores: Ores that contain minerals in the proper portion to undergo smelting without any additional material.

Shaft: A vertical passage in a mine in contrast to a tunnel which is horizontal or sloping downwards. Its function is to hoist or lower men, ore or machinery or ventilate underground workings.

Ship bunkering: The name of the trade by which ships were supplied with coal for steaming purposes.

Shallow diggings: Locations where pay-dirt could be found on or near the surface.

Sinking a shaft: The work of excavating a shaft usually on a vertical plane. The first major project in opening up an underground mine.

Sluice: A wooden trough carrying water and gravel used in the process of placer mining.

Sluice-box: A wooden box in which the gravel is washed for the recovery of gold used in the process of placer mining.

Sluicing: The method by which gravel or sand is carried through sluices and sluice-boxes to recover the gold in placer mining.

Smelter: An establishment in which metals are extracted from their ores.

Smelting: A metallurgical process by which metal is separated from its impurities with which it may be chemically combined or physically mixed.

Smelting flux: Substances which are used in the smelting process to absorb the mineral impurities of a metal.

Stamp: A machine for crushing ore.

Stamp-mill: The building or buildings in which the stamps are housed that crush the ore.

Stope: An excavation underground from which ore has been mined.

Strike: To find a vein of ore or a valuable mineral discovery.

Strata: A geological term for layers of rock.

Strip-mine: An open-pit operation usually made possible by removing the overburden to get at the ore seam by earth moving machinery.

Surface mine: A mine at or near the surface of the ground.

Tailings: Those portions of ore that are regarded as too poor to be treated for further use.

Thermal coal: Coal suitable for use in coal-fired electrical generating plants.

Tipple: A platform from which cars carrying coal from a mine empty the coal into waiting railroad cars or boats.

Tungsten: A hard brittle gray metallic element. Used as filament in electric lamps and as a hardener in the making of high grade steel.

Tunnel: A passageway in the underground workings of a mine. Tunnels are usually built horizontally or sloping downwards in contrast to shafts which are built vertically.

Uranium: A heavy white metallic element which occurs naturally in a number of ores the principal of which is pitchblende. Used in nuclear electrical generating plants.

Water jacketed smelting furnace: A furnace equipped with sections so constructed as to allow free circulation of water to keep it cool.

Water wheel: Used in the early days in the Cariboo to raise water from a creek into flumes for sluicing or hydraulic mining.

Windlass: A cylinder or roller by means of which ore is raised from the shaft of a mine.

Wing dam: A dam built on a bar or creek to expose the bed of the stream. Two or three of these dams would be constructed enclosing an area. The location so dammed off would be pumped dry and then would be mined by rockers and sluices.

Zinc: A bluish-white metallic substance found always combined with other substances in nature. Used in many alloys and in hundreds of industrial products.

INDEX